MICHAEL COHEN'S HOUSE TESTIMONY

THE COMPLETE TRANSCRIPTS AND CASE DOCUMENTS

THE HOUSE COMMITTEE ON OVERSIGHT AND REFORM

DIVERSION
BOOKS

For more information, email info@diversionbooks.com

Diversion Books
A division of Diversion Publishing Corp.
443 Park Avenue South, suite 1004
New York, NY 10016
www.diversionbooks.com

First Diversion Books edition March 2019
Paperback ISBN: 978-1-63576-670-7
eBook ISBN: 978-1-63576-669-1

1 3 5 7 9 10 8 6 4 2

Library of Congress cataloging-in-publication data is available on file.

CONTENTS

UNITED STATES OF AMERICA V. MICHAEL COHEN

THE CHARGES

UNITED STATES DISTRICT COURT
SOUTHERN DISTRICT OF NEW YORK

- - - - - - - - - - - - - - - - - x

UNITED STATES OF AMERICA   :

        - v. -   :

MICHAEL COHEN,   :

        Defendant.   :

                                  :

- - - - - - - - - - - - - - - - - x

INFORMATION

18 Cr.

18 CRIM 850

The Special Counsel charges:

Background

The Defendant

1.   From in or around 2007 through in or around January 2017, MICHAEL COHEN, the defendant, was an attorney and employee of a Manhattan-based real estate company (the "Company"). COHEN held the title of "Executive Vice President" and "Special Counsel" to the owner of the Company ("Individual 1").

False Statements to the U.S. Congress

2.   On or about January 13, 2017, the U.S. Senate Select Committee on Intelligence ("SSCI") announced that it would conduct an investigation into Russian election interference and possible links between Russia and individuals associated with political campaigns. On or about January 25, 2017, the House of Representatives Permanent Select Committee on Intelligence ("HPSCI") announced that it also was conducting an investigation

into Russian election interference and possible links between Russia and individuals associated with political campaigns.

3.   On or about August 28, 2017, COHEN caused a two-page letter to be sent on his behalf to SSCI and HPSCI. The letter addressed his efforts at the Company to pursue a branded property in Moscow, Russia (the "Moscow Project"). COHEN stated the purpose of the letter was "to provide the Committee with additional information regarding the proposal," referring to the Moscow Project.

4.   In the letter to SSCI and HPSCI, COHEN knowingly and deliberately made the following false representations:

   a. **The Moscow Project ended in January 2016 and was not discussed extensively with others in the Company.** "The proposal was under consideration at the [Company] from September 2015 until the end of January 2016. By the end of January 2016, I determined that the proposal was not feasible for a variety of business reasons and should not be pursued further. Based on my business determinations, the [Company] abandoned the [Moscow Project] proposal. . . . To the best of my knowledge, [Individual 1] was never in contact with anyone about this proposal other than me on three occasions. . . . I did not ask or brief [Individual

2

1], or any of his family, before I made the decision to terminate further work on the proposal."

b. **COHEN never agreed to travel to Russia in connection with the Moscow Project and "never considered" asking Individual 1 to travel for the project.** "I primarily communicated with the Moscow-based development company . . . through a U.S. citizen third-party intermediary, [Individual 2]. . . . [Individual 2] constantly asked me to travel to Moscow as part of his efforts to push forward the discussion of the proposal. I ultimately determined that the proposal was not feasible and never agreed to make a trip to Russia. . . . Despite overtures by [Individual 2], I never considered asking [Individual 1] to travel to Russia in connection with this proposal."

c. **COHEN did not recall any Russian government response or contact about the Moscow Project.** "In mid-January 2016, [Individual 2] suggested that I send an email to [Russian Official 1], the Press Secretary for the President of Russia, since the proposal would require approvals within the Russian government that had not been issued. Those permissions were never provided. I decided to abandon the proposal less than two weeks

3

later for business reasons and do not recall any
response to my email, nor any other contacts by me
with [Russian Official 1] or other Russian government
officials about the proposal."

5.   On or about September 19, 2017, COHEN was scheduled to
appear before SSCI accompanied by counsel. In prepared remarks
released to the public, COHEN stated, "I assume we will discuss
the rejected proposal to build a [Company-branded] property in
Moscow that was terminated in January of 2016; which occurred
before the Iowa caucus and months before the very first primary.
This was solely a real estate deal and nothing more. I was doing
my job. I would ask that the two-page statement about the Moscow
proposal that I sent to the Committee in August be incorporated
into and attached to this transcript."

6.   On or about October 25, 2017, COHEN gave testimony to
SSCI, which included testimony about the Moscow Project consistent
with his prepared remarks and his two-page statement.

7.   In truth and in fact, and as COHEN well knew, COHEN's
representations about the Moscow Project he made to SSCI and HPSCI
were false and misleading. COHEN made the false statements to (1)
minimize links between the Moscow Project and Individual 1 and (2)
give the false impression that the Moscow Project ended before
"the Iowa caucus and . . . the very first primary," in hopes of

4

limiting the ongoing Russia investigations. COHEN attempted to
conceal or minimize through his false statements the following
facts:

a. **The Moscow Project was discussed multiple times within
the Company and did not end in January 2016.** Instead,
as late as approximately June 2016, COHEN and
Individual 2 discussed efforts to obtain Russian
governmental approval for the Moscow Project. COHEN
discussed the status and progress of the Moscow
Project with Individual 1 on more than the three
occasions COHEN claimed to the Committee, and he
briefed family members of Individual 1 within the
Company about the project.

b. **COHEN agreed to travel to Russia in connection with
the Moscow Project and took steps in contemplation of
Individual 1's possible travel to Russia.** COHEN and
Individual 2 discussed on multiple occasions
traveling to Russia to pursue the Moscow Project.

i. COHEN asked Individual 1 about the possibility
of Individual 1 traveling to Russia in
connection with the Moscow Project, and asked a
senior campaign official about potential
business travel to Russia.

5

ii.   On or about May 4, 2016, Individual 2 wrote to COHEN, "I had a chat with Moscow. ASSUMING the trip does happen the question is before or after the convention . . . Obviously the pre-meeting trip (you only) can happen anytime you want but the 2 big guys where [sic] the question. I said I would confirm and revert." COHEN responded, "My trip before Cleveland. [Individual 1] once he becomes the nominee after the convention."

iii.   On or about May 5, 2016, Individual 2 followed up with COHEN and wrote, "[Russian Official 1] would like to invite you as his guest to the St. Petersburg Forum which is Russia's Davos it's June 16-19. He wants to meet there with you and possibly introduce you to either [the President of Russia] or [the Prime Minister of Russia], as they are not sure if 1 or both will be there. . . . He said anything you want to discuss including dates and subjects are on the table to discuss."

iv. On or about May 6, 2016, Individual 2 asked COHEN to confirm those dates would work for him to travel. COHEN wrote back, "Works for me."

v. From on or about June 9 to June 14, 2016, Individual 2 sent numerous messages to COHEN about the travel, including forms for COHEN to complete. However, on or about June 14, 2016, COHEN met Individual 2 in the lobby of the Company's headquarters to inform Individual 2 he would not be traveling at that time.

c. **COHEN did recall that in or around January 2016, COHEN received a response from the office of Russian Official 1, the Press Secretary for the President of Russia, and spoke to a member of that office about the Moscow Project.**

i. On or about January 14, 2016, COHEN emailed Russian Official 1's office asking for assistance in connection with the Moscow Project. On or about January 16, 2016, COHEN emailed Russian Official 1's office again, said he was trying to reach another high-level Russian official, and asked for someone who spoke English to contact him.

ii.   On or about January 20, 2016, COHEN received an email from the personal assistant to Russian Official 1 ("Assistant 1"), stating that she had been trying to reach COHEN and requesting that he call her using a Moscow-based phone number she provided.

iii.   Shortly after receiving the email, COHEN called Assistant 1 and spoke to her for approximately 20 minutes. On that call, COHEN described his position at the Company and outlined the proposed Moscow Project, including the Russian development company with which the Company had partnered. COHEN requested assistance in moving the project forward, both in securing land to build the proposed tower and financing the construction. Assistant 1 asked detailed questions and took notes, stating that she would follow up with others in Russia.

iv.   The day after COHEN's call with Assistant 1, Individual 2 contacted him, asking for a call. Individual 2 wrote to COHEN, "It's about [the President of Russia] they called today."

COUNT 1
(False Statements)

8. Paragraphs 1 through 7 of this Information are re-alleged and incorporated by reference as if fully set forth herein.

9. On or about August 28, 2017, the defendant MICHAEL COHEN, in the District of Columbia and elsewhere, in a matter within the jurisdiction of the legislative branch of the Government of the United States, knowingly and willfully made a materially false, fictitious, and fraudulent statement and representation, to wit, COHEN caused to be submitted a written statement to SSCI containing material false statements about the Moscow Project, including false statements about the timing of the Moscow Project, discussions with people in the Company and in Russia about the Moscow Project, and contemplated travel to Russia in connection with the Moscow Project.

(Title 18, United States Code, Section 1001(a)(2).)

ROBERT S. MUELLER, III
Special Counsel

9

UNITED STATES DISTRICT COURT
SOUTHERN DISTRICT OF NEW YORK

UNITED STATES OF AMERICA

- v. -

MICHAEL COHEN,

Defendant.

INFORMATION

18 Cr. ___

ROBERT S. MUELLER, III
SPECIAL COUNSEL

THE PLEA AGREEMENT

NOVEMBER 29, 2018

U.S. Department of Justice

The Special Counsel's Office

Washington, D.C. 20530

November 29, 2018

Guy Petrillo, Esq.
Amy Lester, Esq.
Petrillo Klein & Boxer LLP
655 Third Avenue, 22nd Floor
New York, NY 10017

   Re: <u>United States v. Michael Cohen</u>

Dear Mr. Petrillo and Ms. Lester:

  This letter sets forth the full and complete plea offer to your client, Michael Cohen (hereinafter referred to as "your client" or "defendant"), from the Special Counsel's Office (hereinafter also referred to as "the Government" or "this Office"). If your client accepts the terms and conditions of this offer, please have your client execute this document in the space provided below. Upon receipt of the executed document, this letter will become the Plea Agreement (hereinafter referred to as "this Agreement"). The terms of the offer are as follows:

  1. Charges and Statutory Penalties

  Your client agrees to waive indictment and plead guilty to a Criminal Information, a copy of which is attached, charging your client with making false statements to the U.S. Congress, in violation of 18 U.S.C. § 1001(a)(2).

  Your client understands that a violation of 18 U.S.C. § 1001 carries a maximum sentence of 5 years' imprisonment; a fine of not more than $250,000, pursuant to 18 U.S.C. § 3571(b)(3); a term of supervised release of not more than 3 years, pursuant to 18 U.S.C. § 3583(b)(2); and an obligation to pay any applicable interest or penalties on fines and restitution not timely made.

  In addition, your client agrees to pay a special assessment of $100 per felony conviction to the Clerk of the United States District Court for the Southern District of New York. Your client also understands that, pursuant to 18 U.S.C. § 3572 and § 5E1.2 of the United States Sentencing Commission, *Guidelines Manual* (2017) (hereinafter "Sentencing Guidelines," "Guidelines," or "U.S.S.G."), the Court may also impose a fine that is sufficient to pay the federal government the costs of any imprisonment, term of supervised release, and period of probation.

  2. Plea

  Your client understands and acknowledges that this Agreement is contingent upon the entry of a guilty plea by the defendant in this case. If your client fails to enter a guilty plea, this

Agreement and any proceedings pursuant to this Agreement may be withdrawn or voided in whole or in part at the option of this Office.

3. Factual Stipulations

Your client agrees that the factual allegations found within the Criminal Information fairly and accurately describe your client's actions and involvement in the offense to which your client is pleading guilty.

4. Additional Charges

In consideration of your client's guilty plea to the above offense, your client will not be further prosecuted criminally by this Office for the conduct set forth in the attached Criminal Information; for any other false statements made by him to the U.S. Congress or to this Office in connection with the conduct described in the Criminal Information; and for obstructing, aiding or abetting in the obstruction of, or conspiring to obstruct or commit perjury before congressional or grand jury investigations in connection with the conduct described in the Criminal Information.

5. Sentencing Guidelines Analysis

Your client understands that the sentence in this case will be determined by the Court, pursuant to the factors set forth in 18 U.S.C. § 3553(a), including a consideration of the applicable guidelines and policies set forth in the Sentencing Guidelines. Pursuant to Federal Rule of Criminal Procedure 11(c)(1)(B), and to assist the Court in determining the appropriate sentence, the parties agree to the following:

A. Estimated Offense Level Under the Guidelines

The parties agree that the following Sentencing Guidelines sections apply:

U.S.S.G. § 2B1.1(a)(2)	Base Offense Level:	6
	Total:	6

B. Acceptance of Responsibility

The Government agrees that a 2-level reduction will be appropriate, pursuant to U.S.S.G. § 3E1.1, provided that your client clearly demonstrates acceptance of responsibility, to the satisfaction of the Government, through your client's allocution, adherence to every provision of this Agreement, and conduct between entry of the plea and imposition of sentence.

Nothing in this Agreement limits the right of the Government to seek denial of the adjustment for acceptance of responsibility, pursuant to U.S.S.G. § 3E1.1, and/or imposition of an adjustment for obstruction of justice, pursuant to U.S.S.G. § 3C1.1, regardless of any agreement set forth above, should your client move to withdraw your client's guilty plea after it is entered, or should it be determined by the Government that your client has either (a) engaged in conduct, unknown to the Government at the time of the signing of this Agreement, that constitutes obstruction of justice, (b) engaged in additional criminal conduct after signing this Agreement, or (c) taken any other action inconsistent with acceptance of responsibility.

In accordance with the above, the applicable Guidelines Offense Level will be at least **4**.

C.   Estimated Criminal History Category

Based upon the information now available to this Office, your client was previously convicted in *United States v. Cohen*, No. 1:18-cr-602 (WHP) (S.D.N.Y. Aug. 21, 2018). As of this date, your client has not been sentenced in that matter.

Pursuant to U.S.S.G. § 4A1.1(c) and 4A1.2(a)(4), your client is estimated to have one criminal history point, and your client's Criminal History Category is estimated to be I. Your client acknowledges that if additional convictions are discovered during the pre-sentence investigation by the United States Probation Office, your client's criminal history points may increase.

D.   Estimated Applicable Guidelines Range

Based upon the agreed total offense level and the estimated criminal history category set forth above, your client's estimated Sentencing Guidelines range is zero months to six months' imprisonment (the "Estimated Guidelines Range"). In addition, the parties agree that, pursuant to U.S.S.G. § 5E1.2, should the Court impose a fine, at Guidelines level 4, the estimated applicable fine range is $500 to $9,500. Your client reserves the right to ask the Court not to impose any applicable fine.

The parties agree that, solely for the purposes of calculating the applicable range under the Sentencing Guidelines, neither a downward nor upward departure from the Estimated Guidelines Range set forth above is warranted. Accordingly, neither party will seek any departure or adjustment to the Estimated Guidelines Range, nor will either party suggest that the Court consider such a departure or adjustment, except as provided above. Moreover, your client understands and acknowledges that the Estimated Guidelines Range agreed to by the parties is not binding on the Probation Office or the Court. Should the Court determine that a different guidelines range is applicable, your client will not be permitted to withdraw your client's guilty plea on that basis, and the Government and your client will still be bound by this Agreement.

Your client understands and acknowledges that the terms of this section apply only to conduct that occurred before the execution of this Agreement. Should your client commit any conduct after the execution of this Agreement that would form the basis for an increase in your client's base offense level or justify an upward departure (examples of which include, but are not limited to, obstruction of justice, failure to appear for a court proceeding, criminal conduct while pending sentencing, and false statements to law enforcement agents, the probation officer, or the Court), the Government is free under this Agreement to seek an increase in the base offense level based on that post-agreement conduct.

6.   <u>Agreement under 18 U.S.C. § 3553(a)</u>

Based upon the information known to the Government at the time of the signing of this Agreement, the parties further agree that a sentence within the Estimated Guidelines Range would constitute a reasonable sentence in light of all of the factors set forth in 18 U.S.C. § 3553(a), should such a sentence be subject to appellate review notwithstanding the appeal waiver provided below.

7.   <u>Reservation of Allocution and Cooperation</u>

The Government and your client reserve the right to describe fully, both orally and in writing, to the sentencing judge, the nature and seriousness of your client's misconduct, including any misconduct not described in the charges to which your client is pleading guilty.

The Government agrees to bring to the Court's attention at sentencing in this matter and in *United States v. Cohen*, No. 1:18-cr-602 (WHP) (S.D.N.Y.) the nature and extent of the defendant's cooperation with this Office, on the condition that your client continues to respond and provide truthful information regarding any and all matters as to which this Office deems relevant. The defendant must at all times give complete, truthful, and accurate information and testimony, and must not commit, or attempt to commit, any further crimes.

The Government agrees not to oppose the transfer of this case in its entirety or for the purposes of sentencing to the Judge in *United States v. Cohen*, No. 1:18-cr-602 (WHP) (S.D.N.Y.).

The parties also reserve the right to inform the presentence report writer and the Court of any relevant facts, to dispute any factual inaccuracies in the presentence report, and to contest any matters not provided for in this Agreement. In the event that the Court considers any Sentencing Guidelines adjustments, departures, or calculations different from any agreements contained in this Agreement, or contemplates a sentence outside the Guidelines range based upon the general sentencing factors listed in 18 U.S.C. § 3553(a), the parties reserve the right to answer any related inquiries from the Court. In addition, if in this Agreement the parties have agreed to recommend or refrain from recommending to the Court a particular resolution of any sentencing issue, the parties reserve the right to full allocution in any post-sentence litigation. The parties retain the full right of allocution in connection with any post-sentence motion which may be filed in this matter and/or any proceeding(s) before the Bureau of Prisons. In addition, your client acknowledges that the Government is not obligated and does not intend to file any post-sentence downward departure motion in this case pursuant to Rule 35(b) of the Federal Rules of Criminal Procedure..

8.   <u>Court Not Bound by this Agreement or the Sentencing Guidelines</u>

Your client understands that the sentence in this case will be imposed in accordance with 18 U.S.C. § 3553(a), upon consideration of the Sentencing Guidelines. Your client further understands that the sentence to be imposed is a matter solely within the discretion of the Court. Your client acknowledges that the Court is not obligated to follow any recommendation of the Government at the time of sentencing. Your client understands that neither the Government's recommendation nor the Sentencing Guidelines are binding on the Court.

Your client acknowledges that your client's entry of a guilty plea to the charged offense authorizes the Court to impose any sentence, up to and including the statutory maximum sentence, which may be greater than the applicable Guidelines range. The Government cannot, and does not, make any promise or representation as to what sentence your client will receive. Moreover, it is understood that your client will have no right to withdraw your client's plea of guilty should the Court impose a sentence that is outside the Guidelines range or if the Court does not follow the Government's sentencing recommendation. The Government and your client will be bound by this Agreement, regardless of the sentence imposed by the Court. Any effort by your client to withdraw the guilty plea because of the length of the sentence shall constitute a breach of this Agreement.

9.   **Waivers**

   A.   **Venue**

Your client waives any challenge to venue in the Southern District of New York.

   B.   **Statute of Limitations**

Your client agrees that, should the conviction following your client's plea of guilty pursuant to this Agreement be vacated for any reason, any prosecution, based on the conduct set forth in the attached Criminal Information, that is not time-barred by the applicable statute of limitations on the date of the signing of this Agreement (including any counts that the Government has agreed not to prosecute or to dismiss at sentencing pursuant to this Agreement) may be commenced or reinstated against your client, notwithstanding the expiration of the statute of limitations between the signing of this Agreement and the commencement or reinstatement of such prosecution. It is the intent of this Agreement to waive all defenses based on the statute of limitations with respect to any prosecution of conduct set forth in the attached Criminal Information that is not time-barred on the date that this Agreement is signed.

   C.   **Trial Rights**

Your client understands that by pleading guilty in this case your client agrees to waive certain rights afforded by the Constitution of the United States and/or by statute or rule. Your client agrees to forego the right to any further discovery or disclosures of information not already provided at the time of the entry of your client's guilty plea. Your client also agrees to waive, among other rights, the right to be indicted by a Grand Jury, the right to plead not guilty, and the right to a jury trial. If there were a jury trial, your client would have the right to be represented by counsel, to confront and cross-examine witnesses against your client, to challenge the admissibility of evidence offered against your client, to compel witnesses to appear for the purpose of testifying and presenting other evidence on your client's behalf, and to choose whether to testify. If there were a jury trial and your client chose not to testify at that trial, your client would have the right to have the jury instructed that your client's failure to testify could not be held against your client. Your client would further have the right to have the jury instructed that your client is presumed innocent until proven guilty, and that the burden would be on the United States to prove your client's guilt beyond a reasonable doubt. If your client were found guilty after a trial, your client would have the right to appeal your client's conviction. Your client understands that the Fifth Amendment to the Constitution of the United States protects your client from the use of self-incriminating statements in a criminal prosecution. By entering a plea of guilty, your client knowingly and voluntarily waives or gives up your client's right against self-incrimination.

Your client acknowledges discussing with you Rule 11(f) of the Federal Rules of Criminal Procedure and Rule 410 of the Federal Rules of Evidence, which ordinarily limit the admissibility of statements made by a defendant in the course of plea discussions or plea proceedings if a guilty plea is later withdrawn. Your client knowingly and voluntarily waives the rights that arise under these rules in the event your client withdraws your client's guilty plea or withdraws from this Agreement after signing it.

Your client also agrees to waive all constitutional and statutory rights to a speedy sentence and agrees that the plea of guilty pursuant to this Agreement will be entered at a time decided upon by the parties with the concurrence of the Court. Your client understands that the date for sentencing will be set by the Court.

D. Appeal Rights

Your client understands that federal law, specifically 18 U.S.C. § 3742, affords defendants the right to appeal their sentences in certain circumstances. Your client agrees to waive the right to appeal the sentence in this case, including but not limited to any term of imprisonment, fine, forfeiture, award of restitution, term or condition of supervised release, authority of the Court to set conditions of release, and the manner in which the sentence was determined, except to the extent the Court sentences your client above the statutory maximum or guidelines range determined by the Court or your client claims that your client received ineffective assistance of counsel, in which case your client would have the right to appeal the illegal sentence or above-guidelines sentence or raise on appeal a claim of ineffective assistance of counsel, but not to raise on appeal other issues regarding the sentencing. In agreeing to this waiver, your client is aware that your client's sentence has yet to be determined by the Court. Realizing the uncertainty in estimating what sentence the Court ultimately will impose, your client knowingly and willingly waives your client's right to appeal the sentence, to the extent noted above, in exchange for the concessions made by the Government in this Agreement.

E. Collateral Attack

Your client also waives any right to challenge the conviction entered or sentence imposed under this Agreement or otherwise attempt to modify or change the sentence or the manner in which it was determined in any collateral attack, including, but not limited to, a motion brought under 28 U.S.C. § 2255 or Federal Rule of Civil Procedure 60(b), except to the extent such a motion is based on newly discovered evidence or on a claim that your client received ineffective assistance of counsel. Your client reserves the right to file a motion brought under 18 U.S.C. § 3582(c)(2), but agrees to waive the right to appeal the denial of such a motion.

F. Privacy Act and FOIA Rights

Your client also agrees to waive all rights, whether asserted directly or by a representative, to request or receive from any department or agency of the United States any records pertaining to the investigation or prosecution of this case, including and without limitation any records that may be sought under the Freedom of Information Act, 5 U.S.C. § 552, or the Privacy Act, 5 U.S.C. § 552a, for the duration of the Office's investigation.

10. Restitution

Your client understands that the Court has an obligation to determine whether, and in what amount, mandatory restitution applies in this case under 18 U.S.C. § 3663A. The Government and your client agree that mandatory restitution does not apply in this case.

11. Breach of Agreement

Your client understands and agrees that, if after entering this Agreement, your client fails specifically to perform or to fulfill completely each and every one of your client's obligations under this Agreement, or engages in any criminal activity prior to sentencing, your client will have breached this Agreement. In the event of such a breach: (a) the Government will be free from its obligations under this Agreement; (b) your client will not have the right to withdraw the guilty plea; (c) your client will be fully subject to criminal prosecution for any other crimes, including perjury and obstruction of justice; and (d) the Government will be free to use against your client, directly and indirectly, in any criminal or civil proceeding, all statements made by your client and any of the information or materials provided by your client, including such statements, information and materials provided pursuant to this Agreement or during the course of any debriefings conducted in anticipation of, or after entry of, this Agreement, whether or not the debriefings were previously characterized as "off-the-record" debriefings, and including your client's statements made during proceedings before the Court pursuant to Rule 11 of the Federal Rules of Criminal Procedure.

Your client understands and agrees that the Government shall be required to prove a breach of this Agreement only by a preponderance of the evidence, except where such breach is based on a violation of federal, state, or local criminal law, which the Government need prove only by probable cause in order to establish a breach of this Agreement.

Nothing in this Agreement shall be construed to permit your client to commit perjury, to make false statements or declarations, to obstruct justice, or to protect your client from prosecution for any crimes not included within this Agreement or committed by your client after the execution of this Agreement. Your client understands and agrees that the Government reserves the right to prosecute your client for any such offenses. Your client further understands that any perjury, false statements or declarations, or obstruction of justice relating to your client's obligations under this Agreement that takes place after execution of this Agreement shall constitute a breach of this Agreement. In the event of such a breach, your client will not be allowed to withdraw your client's guilty plea.

12.   Complete Agreement

Other than a proffer agreement executed on August 7, 2018 and continued on September 12, September 18, October 8, October 17, November 12, and November 20, 2018, no agreements, promises, understandings, or representations have been made by the parties or their counsel other than those contained in writing herein, nor will any such agreements, promises, understandings, or representations be made unless committed to writing and signed by your client, defense counsel, and the Office. The proffer agreement, with respect to the Government, is superseded as noticed herein if the Agreement is breached.

This Office recognizes that, in connection with this Agreement, the defendant is entering into an agreement with the U.S. Attorney's Office for the Southern District of New York concerning the potential effect of this Agreement on the sentencing in *United States v. Cohen*, No. 1:18-cr-602 (WHP) (S.D.N.Y.).

Your client further understands that other than as set forth herein, this Agreement is binding only upon the Office, and does not bind any other United States Attorney's Office, nor does it bind any other state, local, or federal prosecutor. It also does not bar or compromise any civil, tax, or administrative claim pending or that may be made against your client.

If the foregoing terms and conditions are satisfactory, your client may so indicate by signing this Agreement no later than November 29, 2018.

Sincerely yours,

ROBERT S. MUELLER, III
Special Counsel

By: _____

Jeannie S. Rhee
Andrew D. Goldstein
L. Rush Atkinson
The Special Counsel's Office

DEFENDANT'S ACCEPTANCE

I have read every page of this Agreement and have discussed it with my attorneys, Guy Petrillo and Amy Lester. I fully understand this Agreement and agree to it without reservation. I do this voluntarily and of my own free will, intending to be legally bound. No threats have been made to me nor am I under the influence of anything that could impede my ability to understand this Agreement fully. I am pleading guilty because I am in fact guilty of the offense identified in this Agreement.

I reaffirm that absolutely no promises, agreements, understandings, or conditions have been made or entered into in connection with my decision to plead guilty except those set forth in this Agreement. I am satisfied with the legal services provided by my attorneys in connection with this Agreement and matters related to it.

Date: 11/28/18

Michael Cohen
Defendant

ATTORNEY'S ACKNOWLEDGMENT

I have read every page of this Agreement, reviewed this Agreement with my client, Michael Cohen, and fully discussed the provisions of this Agreement with my client. These pages accurately and completely set forth the entire Agreement.

Date: 11-29-18

Guy Petrillo, Esq.
Amy Lester, Esq.
Attorneys for Defendant

Page **9** of **9**

THE COURT PROCEEDINGS

DECEMBER 12, 2018

1   UNITED STATES DISTRICT COURT
    SOUTHERN DISTRICT OF NEW YORK
2   ------------------------------x
    UNITED STATES OF AMERICA
3   v.   18 CR 602 (WHP)
                                           18 CR 850 (WHP)
4   Sentence
    MICHAEL COHEN
5
                   Defendant
6   ------------------------------x

7   New York, N.Y.
                                           December 12, 2018
8   11:00 a.m.

9   Before:
                    HON. WILLIAM H. PAULEY III
10   District Judge

11
                           APPEARANCES
12 GEOFFREY S. BERMAN
         United States Attorney for the
13   Southern District of New York
    NICHOLAS ROOS
14 THOMAS McKAY
    RACHEL MAIMIN
15 ANDREA GRISWOLD
         Assistant United States Attorneys
16

17 UNITED STATES DEPARTMENT OF JUSTICE
         Special Counsel's Office
18 JEANNIE S. RHEE
    ANDREW D. GOLDSTEIN
19 L. RUSH ATKINSON
         Assistant United States Attorneys
20

21 PETRILLO KLEIN & BOXER LLP
         Attorneys for Defendant
22 GUY PETRILLO
    AMY LESTER
23
    -Also Present-
24 HEATHER D'AGOSTINO, FBI
    MICKEY ROBINSON, FBI
25

ICCQCOHs

1   (Case called)

2   DEPUTY CLERK: Appearances for the United States

3   Attorney's Office.

4   MR. ROOS: For the United States Attorney's Office,

5   good morning.

6   Nicks Roos, Thomas McKay, Rachel Maimin and Andrea

7   Griswold.

8   DEPUTY CLERK: Appearances for Special Counsel's

9   Office.

10   MS. RHEE: Jeannie Rhee on behalf of Special Counsel's

11   Office. I'm joined here today by Andrew Goldstein and Rush

12   Atkinson. Also in the courtroom in the back, we're joined by

13   FBI Heather D'Agostino and Mickey Robinson.

14   DEPUTY CLERK: Appearances for the defendant.

15   MR. PETRILLO: Good morning, your Honor.

16   Guy Petrillo and Amy Lester for Michael Cohen.

17   THE COURT: Good morning to all of you, and I note the

18   presence of the defendant, Mr. Cohen, at counsel table.

19   This matter is on for sentencing. Are the parties

20   ready to proceed?

21   MR. ROOS: Yes, your Honor.

22   MR. PETRILLO: Yes, your Honor.

23   MS. RHEE: Yes, your Honor.

24   THE COURT: First, Mr. Petrillo, have you reviewed

25   with your client the presentence investigation report?

ICCQCOHs

1   MR. PETRILLO: I have, your Honor.

2   THE COURT: Are there any factual matters set forth in

3   the report that you believe warrant modification or correction?

4   MR. PETRILLO: Not at this time, your Honor. Thank

5   you.

6   THE COURT: Mr. Roos, are there any factual matters

7   set forth in the presentence report that the government

8   believes warrant modification or correction?

9   MR. ROOS: No, your Honor.

10   THE COURT: What about the Special Counsel's Office?

11   MS. RHEE: No, your Honor.

12   THE COURT: Very well.

13   MR. PETRILLO: Your Honor, just to confirm, did the

14   Court receive our letter of last night?

15   THE COURT: I did.

16   MR. PETRILLO: Very well.

17   THE COURT: I did.

18   Now, the parties here, before I hear from them, have a

19   difference of opinion concerning the guidelines calculation,

20   and, in particular, the grouping analysis for 18 CR 602.

21   Defense counsel argues that the tax evasion counts are

22   not closely related to the other counts and, therefore, should

23   not be grouped together. The government counters that Section

24   3D1.2 specifically enumerates guidelines that are to be

25   grouped, which include Section 2T1.1 for the tax evasion

ICCQCOHs

1   counts, Section 2B1.1 for the false statement count, and

2   Section 2C1.8 for the illegal campaign contributions counts.

3   This Court finds the government's argument to be

4   correct as a matter of law where the offense levels are

5   principally determined by the amount of loss. *See United*

6   *States v. Gordon*, 291 F.3d 181, 192 (2d.Cir 2002).

7   Accordingly, this Court makes the following guidelines

8   calculations: Grouping all eight counts of 18 CR 602 together,

9   the base offense level is 7. Because the loss here exceeded

10 $1.5 million, but was less than $3.5 million, an increase of 16

11 levels is warranted.

12   Further, because the offense involved the use of

13 sophisticated means, including Mr. Cohen's creation of shell

14 companies and fake invoices, a further two-level enhancement is

15 appropriate.

16   Finally, because Mr. Cohen used special skills as a

17 licensed attorney to facilitate the commission and concealment

18 of these offenses, a further two-level enhancement is

19 warranted. Thus, the adjusted offense level for group one,

20 that is, the counts charged in 18 CR 602, is 27.

21   Now, Mr. Cohen pled guilty to these crimes in a timely

22 manner before me and, accordingly, I grant him a three-level

23 reduction for acceptance of responsibility. Thus, his total

24 offense level is 24. The defendant has no prior criminal

25 convictions, and, therefore, his Criminal History Category is a

ICCQCOHs

1   I. With a total offense level of 24 and a Criminal History

2   Category of I, Mr. Cohen's guideline range is 51 to 63 months

3   of imprisonment on the eight charges of income tax evasion,

4   making false statements to a banking institution, and the two

5   campaign finance crimes.

6   Now, with respect to Mr. Cohen's plea to making false

7   statements to Congress, that is separately grouped and has a

8   base offense level of 6. This Court agrees with the Special

9   Counsel's Office and Mr. Cohen that no enhancements are

10   appropriate. Mr. Cohen pled guilty to this crime before my

11   colleague, Judge Carter, and, accordingly, I grant him a

12   two-level reduction for acceptance of responsibility on this

13   offense. So, with a total offense level of 4 and a Criminal

14   History Category of I, his guidelines range for making false

15   statements to Congress is zero to six months of imprisonment.

16   Accordingly, no multiple account adjustment applies.

17   And so with the guidelines calculation resolved, I

18   will hear now from the parties.

19   Mr. Petrillo, do you wish to be heard on behalf of

20   Mr. Cohen?

21   MR. PETRILLO: I do, your Honor. Thank you.

22   Your Honor, may it please the Court, thank you.

23   My partner, Amy Lester, and I have the privilege of

24   representing Michael Cohen and the honor of having met some of

25   the members of his family who are present here today. The

ICCQCOHs

1   group is larger than I've met, but it includes his mother and
2   father, his mother-in-law and his father-in-law, his wife and
3   children, and his brother and sisters, along with a niece and a
4   cousin.

5   Your Honor, we have made a sentencing submission with
6   numerous letters in support of the character of Mr. Cohen, and
7   it would not be our purpose today to repeat all of what we have
8   already written. Rather, unless your Honor would like me to
9   proceed otherwise, I would like first to address the remarkable
10 nature and significance of the life decision made by Mr. Cohen
11 to cooperate with the DOJ Special Counsel and the relevance
12 and, respectfully, the importance of that cooperation, not only
13 to this specific man and your Honor's evaluation of this
14 specific man, but also to the Court's consideration of how
15 Mr. Cohen's cooperation promotes respect for law and the
16 courage of the individual to stand up to power and influence.

17   When Mr. Cohen authorized us to contact the Special
18 Counsel's Office in July, he did so to offer his relevant
19 knowledge to the investigation knowing that he would face as a
20 result when his offer became public a barrage of attack by the
21 President. He knew that the President might shut down the
22 investigation, and he knew that there might come a time when he
23 would appear in court, and there would be no Special Counsel to
24 stand up for him, as there is today.

25   He moved forward nonetheless. So it is true, as has

ICCQCOHs

1   been pointed out by the government, that part of what Mr. Cohen

2   did in coming forward is similar to what many folks who are

3   expecting criminal charges do in that expectation. At that

4   time he acknowledged that it was more than possible that his

5   case might proceed from mere investigation to charges and that

6   his offer to assist could help him in some fashion should there

7   be charges and should there be a proceeding. But it is also

8   the case that his decision was an importantly different

9   decision from the usual decision to cooperate. He came forward

10   to offer evidence against the most powerful person in our

11   country. He did so not knowing what the result would be, not

12   knowing how the politics would play out, and not knowing

13   whether the Special Counsel would even survive, nor could he

14   anticipate the full measure of attack that has been made

15   against him; not only by the President, who continues to say

16   that people like Mr. Cohen who cooperate with the Special

17   Counsel are weaklings and those who hold fast and clam up are

18   heroes, but also attacks by partisans and by citizens who

19   happen to be aligned with the President. And those attacks

20   have included threats against him and his family.

21   So, respectfully, this is not a standard case of

22   cooperation. The cooperation here should be viewed under a

23   non-standard or in a non-standard framework. The SCO's

24   investigation, the Special Counsel's investigation is of the

25   utmost national significance, no less than seen 40 plus years

ICCQCOHs

1   ago in the days of Watergate. In the light of that reality,

2   respectfully, your Honor, it is important that others in

3   Mr. Cohen's position who provide assistance to this historic

4   inquiry take renewed courage from this proceeding, and that law

5   enforcement and the promotion of respect for law also receive a

6   boost from what happens here today. Mr. Cohen would want me to

7   say that he's always respected law enforcement. He's always

8   supported it.

9   In the plea agreement with the Special Counsel, the

10   Special Counsel committed, subject to conditions that have been

11   fully satisfied, to bring to your Honor's attention for

12   sentencing purposes in both cases the nature and extent of

13   Mr. Cohen's cooperation with that office. The Special Counsel

14   says Mr. Cohen has gone to significant lengths to assist the

15   investigation, providing information on core topics under

16   investigation, and is committed to continue to assist.

17   The office says the information provided has been

18   credible and consistent with other evidence obtained in its

19   investigation. The office further says that it has been useful

20   cooperation in four specific respects that are detailed in the

21   Special Counsel letter to the Court. And, finally, Mr. Cohen,

22   according to the Special Counsel, has made substantial and

23   significant efforts to remediate his own misconduct, accept

24   responsibility for his actions, and assist the Special

25   Counsel's investigation.

ICCQCOHs

1   Even the Southern District which has submitted a

2 somewhat sharp memo, which I will comment on in a few minutes,

3 to the Court, agrees that Mr. Cohen's assistance to the Special

4 Counsel was significant. That's at page 17 of its memo. And

5 that his provision of information to law enforcement in matters

6 of national interest is deserving of credit. And that's at

7 page 37 of the memo.

8   Your Honor, in this exceptionally important matter,

9 Mr. Cohen's cooperation is overwhelmingly the factor, we

10 submit, that should substantially mitigate his sentence, and

11 his action stands in profound contrast to the decision of some

12 others not to cooperate and allegedly to double deal while

13 pretending to cooperate.

14   But that's not all. We also ask the Court

15 respectfully that it consider Mr. Cohen's life of good works as

16 it considers the sentence in this case. As we set forth in our

17 memo, and as supported by the letters sent with the memo, he

18 has been a prodigious fundraiser for the St. Jude's Children's

19 Hospital.

20   He has been the key figure at a Manhattan private

21 school in the raising of funds committed to financial aid for

22 students without means to attend and who otherwise would not be

23 able to attend absent his efforts.

24   He has done likewise impressive fundraising for

25 Operation Smile and assisted the Weatherford Foundation with

ICCQCOHs

1 active personal efforts to advance the role model program of

2 that athletes' organization.

3 Your Honor has read, I have no doubt, of the aid and

4 assistance Mr. Cohen provides regularly to children and friends

5 when they need to find medical care and stands by them in their

6 times of illness and hard times.

7 Whatever millions of words are said and written about

8 Mr. Cohen, and certainly he's in the paper every day, and on TV

9 there's coverage, sometimes it appears 24/7, this is a man of

10 generous spirit and the submissions to the Court demonstrate

11 that.

12 There is some mention in the Southern District's memo

13 regarding emphasis on his own contributions financially, but I

14 don't find it in our memo. The crux of what we're saying is

15 that he puts himself out to raise money for very, very

16 worthwhile organizations. He puts his whole body into it, and

17 this is a man whose first instinct is to help.

18 When it comes to Mr. Cohen's capacity to follow

19 through in his commitment to lead a good and law-abiding life,

20 I would also like to underscore what the Court has been

21 informed of by several members of the bar. All portray a man

22 of integrity and honorable intentions and care for the

23 underserved, a man who does not engage in sharp business

24 practices.

25 To be sure, the Southern District points out that like

ICCQCOHs

1 many clients that lawyers meet from time to time, Mr. Cohen has

2 occasionally erupted in frustration at what he perceives to be

3 wrongs. For example, as the Southern District points out, he

4 became very angry when a bank refused to focus on a transaction

5 that would have allowed him to sell his taxi medallions at a

6 time when doing so would have been lucrative, waited so long

7 before they approved the transactions, that the transaction

8 melted away as the market dipped. He expressed frustration,

9 and that is cited in the Southern District's memo as evidence

10 of a bad character. I have so many clients who come into my

11 office on a regular basis frustrated with life. That's an

12 immature and meaningless observation in my view as to his

13 character. It's simplistic and it's unfair.

14   Mr. Alpstein says, a lawyer who's worked with

15 Mr. Cohen on transactions, "Every seller of a transaction on

16 which I've represented Michael would say without equivocation

17 that Michael was and is an honest, responsible, and fair

18 businessman."

19   The man is 52 years old. There's a long record of how

20 he has conducted himself in business and with financial

21 institutions. No bank has ever lost money dealing with Michael

22 Cohen. I'll say that again: No bank has ever lost money

23 dealing with Michael Cohen. No friend in need has ever been

24 turned away.

25   Your Honor, we addressed the offense conduct, and I

ICCQCOHs

1 had not planned to say more than a few words about it until I

2 read the Southern District's memo, and I just want to say few

3 words in response to the memo. And I don't want to belabor it;

4 I know that you've read all the materials. No one is saying,

5 least of all, Michael Cohen, or has said that a false statement

6 to a bank is other than serious. In this case, we simply made

7 the point that the home equity line of credit as to which the

8 application was false was ten times oversecured at the time of

9 the application and that no money damage resulted. Does that

10 make it right? No. It does not make it right. But it puts

11 the conduct into some kind of proportion.

12   No one is saying, least of us, Michael Cohen, that tax

13 evasion of any kind is other than serious. The speaking

14 information in this case, however, says that the crux of the

15 conduct was failing to identify deposits as income to an

16 accountant who received bank statements. Does that make it

17 right? No. It doesn't make it right. But it puts in

18 proportion and points out that the Court here is not dealing

19 with a mastermind of tax deception.

20   Ms. Lester and I were given three to four days to

21 speak to the tax charges in this case before they were filed.

22 They were not specified. When asked questions about what they

23 entailed, I was met with stony silence and no realistic

24 opportunity to meet with the tax division, as is common. I

25 believe that we would have had a very strong chance of

ICCQCOHs

1 diverting the case from the criminal track had we had that

2 opportunity.

3   But life is tough and Michael Cohen accepts that. We

4 accept it. Our point is not to explain the conduct away. Our

5 point is to say that the offense is well within the heartland

6 of cases that are routinely treated in a non-criminal context,

7 solely so that your Honor can consider the punishment aspect

8 associated with the criminal tax evasion that has been

9 admitted, and that no one is trying to push away as someone

10 else's fault.

11   I will say very little on the campaign charges, the

12 campaign finance charges, and the statement to the legislature.

13 I do want to point out what Mr. Gerber, a lawyer in New York,

14 writes to the Court. He's a former member of the grievance

15 committee, and he's written on behalf of Mr. Cohen that he's

16 seen many attorneys succumb to the wishes of a particularly

17 persuasive client. "Mr. Cohen," he writes, "had a client whose

18 extraordinary power of persuasion got him elected to the

19 highest office in the land." Again, the conduct is quite

20 serious, but Mr. Gerber's experience is certainly worthy of

21 note, as the Court takes into account the human element of what

22 happened here.

23   Based on all these factors, your Honor, most

24 importantly cooperation, good works, and the nature of the

25 offenses, we respectfully submit that the case calls for a full

ICCQCOHs

1 consideration of mercy as your Honor sentences our client,

2 Michael Cohen.

3   A few words on what the Southern District has

4 submitted. It is not the case that Mr. Cohen has declined to

5 answer questions from the Southern District or from our duly

6 authorized U.S. Attorney's Offices, state law enforcement

7 entities, and Congress. He's ready to do that. He is wary of

8 a long-term cooperation agreement for personal reasons and

9 because he wants both to remove himself and to remove his

10 family from the glare of the cameras and try to work his way

11 and their way back from an abnormal life. The period of such

12 an agreement would be indeterminate. The press is overwhelming

13 in this case. But none of this is to say he will not make

14 himself available for questioning on investigated matters, and

15 indeed, as you know, he's already met with the Southern

16 District on one of those matters.

17   But it's also unfair and it's mere innuendo that

18 Mr. Cohen would not describe his own misconduct, as the

19 government says twice, "if any." I know the Court is aware

20 that search warrants were executed in this case. As a result,

21 all of his papers, computers, devices, phones, and recordings

22 were seized and dozens of agents, and at least four Assistant

23 U.S. Attorneys and supervisors questioned dozens and dozens of

24 witnesses and reviewed the evidence. They know what is there.

25 He pled to what he pled to, and the plea agreement immunized

ICCQCOHs

1   him for the conduct that the plea agreement immunized him for.

2   When the government repeats twice that Mr. Cohen declined to

3   disclose his prior bad acts "if any," they come forward with

4   nothing to suggest that they don't know everything already,

5   much less that there's anything there.

6   At the end of the day, it's not that important, your

7   Honor. I just don't think it's fair. I don't really

8   understand the strident tone of the memo, and trying to put it

9   into context, I'm looking at the beginning of the case. First,

10 an unwillingness to delineate charges, a claim that I should

11 already know what they are. A few days to respond once three

12 categories of alleged offenses were set forth. And then after

13 the plea, a courthouse press conference on a plea of guilty. I

14 submit, your Honor, that no other defendant would be treated in

15 this fashion on these offenses, but Mr. Cohen had the

16 misfortune to have been counsel to the President.

17   This rush to charge and media display suggest,

18 respectfully, that the Court should take with a healthy grain

19 of salt the contentions by the Southern District of New York

20 that Mr. Cohen left them at the altar of a Southern District

21 cooperation agreement. Rather, he made a personal and rational

22 decision that he would respond truthfully to any investigative

23 topic, but that it was not in his or his family's interest to

24 remain in the constant glare and under the requirements of a

25 cooperation agreement which could go on for months and months

1   and years and years. And he sat down with Southern, and they
2   found him "forthright and credible." Page 15.
3   The rules of the Southern District of New York as to
4   how every case of cooperation should proceed, of course, were
5   given to us by the minor gods and woe unto those who fail to
6   follow their scriptures, but they don't mean that they work in
7   every situation, no matter the facts, no matter the
8   circumstances. They don't mean the prosecutor is always right
9   about how the standard procedure will play out.
10   And, effectively, your Honor, the Southern District
11   would have this Court penalize Mr. Cohen because he did not
12   follow their standard form agreement and procedure even though
13   he cooperated with the Special Counsel, provided them with
14   forthright and credible information, and offered, and hereby
15   offers, to respond to any other questions, and they would do it
16   without putting forth anything to suggest that there's any
17   there there by way of prior bad acts. This approach, your
18   Honor, is erroneous. It's error to consider what they are
19   asking you to consider. It's fundamentally unfair for a
20   prosecutor to ask a Court to sentence a defendant on
21   hypothetical facts and circumstances rather than based on the
22   facts and circumstances that the Court actually knows. Those
23   facts and circumstances do not present a mystery of the kind
24   that the office's memorandum seeks to suggest. I don't know
25   what's behind it, and it's peculiar in a context in which a

ICCQCOHs

1   sibling office of the DOJ agrees that Mr. Cohen cooperated as

2   set forth in the plea agreement and as reported to your Honor

3   in the Special Counsel's letter.

4   I'm not going to overly speculate about what's going

5   on here. I think the Court has as much experience as I in

6   these matters, but I would suggest that power to the Southern

7   District if they want to make a bigger case than they've

8   already made, God bless them. And maybe there's a little bit

9   of pride involved here in not being at the center of attention.

10   Who knows? Maybe all those articles about a big financial

11   fraud case and a big taxi medallion case followed by these

12   pleas is somehow disappointing. It's not for me to say.

13   We respectfully request, your Honor, a variance under

14   the guidelines and the exercise of leniency in the imposition

15   of sentence on Mr. Cohen, and we request that on behalf of our

16   client and his family. He has done, Michael has, a good deal

17   to help, not only the Special Counsel but a lot of people. He

18   is a very good man.

19   Thank you.

20   THE COURT: Thank you, Mr. Petrillo.

21   Ms. Rhee, does the Special Counsel's Office wish to be

22   heard?

23   MS. RHEE: Yes, your Honor.

24   Thank you, your Honor. On behalf of the Special

25   Counsel's Office, our remarks will be brief. We rely, and we

ICCQCOHs

1   speak primarily through our written submission which has

2   already been submitted to this Court. In supplement to that,

3   we just have two discrete, important points that we want to

4   highlight for the Court's attention.

5   The first is that the offense that Mr. Cohen pled to

6   in 18 CR 850 was a serious criminal violation. As Mr. Petrillo

7   alluded to, the subject at issue here that Mr. Cohen actively

8   misled Congress about was an issue of national importance and

9   interest, and Mr. Cohen intentionally repeated many of the

10   false statements to us at the Special Counsel's Office

11   initially when we met with him in July. And those false

12   statements were intended to limit ongoing investigations into

13   Russian interference in a U.S. presidential election, and the

14   question of any links or coordination between a campaign and a

15   foreign government. Our submission elucidates why those lies

16   were material, why those lies were consequential.

17   But what we really want to leave with the Court today

18   for the Court's consideration is Mr. Cohen's interactions with

19   the Special Counsel's Office since that initial voluntary

20   interview in July. The government has agreed with Mr. Cohen to

21   bring his assistance to your attention for due consideration at

22   this sentencing, and what we want to say about that is that

23   Mr. Cohen has endeavored from his second session with us in

24   September of this year going forward to this day, he has

25   endeavored to account for his criminal misconduct in numerous

ICCQCOHs

1   ways. He has fully accepted responsibility for the lies that

2   he told Congress. He has provided our office with credible and

3   reliable information about core Russia-related issues under

4   investigation and within the purview of the Special Counsel's

5   Office. There is only so much that we can say about the

6   particulars at this time given our ongoing investigation, but

7   we hope that we have sufficiently outlined for the Court that

8   they were ranging, and that they were helpful.

9   Finally, your Honor, what we want to highlight for

10 this Court is that one of the things that we and the Special

11 Counsel's Office have most appreciated about Mr. Cohen's

12 assistance is that he has provided valuable information,

13 investigative information, to us while taking care and being

14 careful to note what he knows and what he doesn't know. Rather

15 than inflate the value of any information that he has brought

16 forward to us in what he had to provide, Mr. Cohen has sought

17 to tell us the truth, and that is of utmost value to us as we

18 seek in our office to determine what in fact occurred.

19   And so we want to highlight that for the Court and to

20 underscore what we set out in our submission about the value,

21 the nature, the reliability, and the credibility of Mr. Cohen's

22 assistance.

23   THE COURT: Thank you, Ms. Rhee.

24   MS. RHEE: Thank you, your Honor.

25   THE COURT: Mr. Roos, does the United States

1 Attorney's Office wish to be heard?

2   MR. ROOS: Yes, your Honor. Thank you.

3   Your Honor, I'd like to start where Mr. Petrillo

4 ended, which is to share a few words about the information that

5 Mr. Cohen provided to law enforcement and the credit that is

6 appropriate.

7   Now, we agree that Mr. Cohen's decision to provide

8 information to the Special Counsel's Office in matters of

9 national interest is deserving of credit, and we defer to SCO's

10 description of Mr. Cohen's assistance to them and in their

11 investigation. We don't dispute any of that assessment or the

12 assessment, frankly, that defense counsel has made.

13   But for the reasons that we've detailed in our

14 sentencing memorandum, any downward variance that Mr. Cohen

15 receives should be modest. Any successful assistance Mr. Cohen

16 provided was in the context of a case where the guidelines

17 range is zero to six months. It's within the context of the

18 Special Counsel Office's case.

19   But here, he is facing three additional categories of

20 crimes, eight total charges, and didn't come anywhere close to

21 assisting this office in an investigation. There is no mystery

22 about this. No one is attempting to penalize Mr. Cohen for not

23 cooperating. Quite the opposite, there is no obligation to

24 cooperate, but for all the hypothesizing that Mr. Petrillo has

25 done, Mr. Cohen can't have it both ways. There is a standard

ICCQCOHs

1   way in which this office conducts cooperation. Your Honor is

2   familiar with it. There is no reason, no matter the

3   significance or the nature of the case, whether or not it

4   receives public attention, for us to depart from that practice.

5   We've treated Mr. Cohen just the way we treat every other

6   defendant that deals with the United States Attorney's Office.

7   Now, Mr. Cohen, he chose not to pursue the path of

8   full cooperation. He didn't provide substantial assistance to

9   the government in this investigation, and he doesn't have a 5K

10 letter. And for these reasons, our view is that a significant

11 variance, the variance urged by the defendant isn't warranted

12 here. To do so would send the wrong message. It would send

13 the message that a defendant who chooses a different path, a

14 selective cooperation on only particular subjects can receive

15 the credit that so many defendants seek when they expose

16 themselves completely to the government.

17   Now, I'd like to touch on two points, two of the

18 3553(a) factors that in the government's view are so important

19 here, and they really go to what Mr. Petrillo said about the

20 nature and the seriousness of these offenses.

21   So, first, the defendant pled guilty to four crimes

22 here, your Honor, and Mr. Petrillo, he identified areas in

23 which certain crimes in their view may not be as serious, but

24 he pled guilty to four different crimes, and your Honor is

25 sentencing Mr. Cohen not only on four different charges but

ICCQCOHs

1   four separate crimes. Each of those charges is itself serious.

2   Each merits punishment in its own right. Each cause a distinct

3   harm, and taken together there is a compounding effect.

4   Collectively, the charges portray a pattern of deception, of

5   brazenness, and of greed that manifested in multiple aspects of

6   Mr. Cohen's professional life.

7   In particular, Mr. Cohen's conduct related to the

8   election is serious because of the tremendous societal cost

9   associated with the campaign finance crimes and the lies to

10   Congress. Mr. Cohen committed these deceptive acts to protect

11   the political campaign from allegations of impropriety, and, by

12   his own admission, he committed the campaign finance crimes for

13   the purpose of influencing the election.

14   He also, quite brazenly, stole millions of dollars in

15   income from the IRS. And on this subject, defense counsel

16   describes the ways in which this is really nothing more than a

17   civil matter. But that is not the case, your Honor. These tax

18   crimes went on for at least five years. They involve millions

19   of dollars of income that was deliberately not reported to the

20   IRS. This is not a case of an assessed tax not being paid.

21   It's something quite different. It was deliberate, it was

22   willful, and that's what the defendant's plea reflects.

23   Now, together these crimes implicate core defining

24   parts of our democracy: Government funded by the people, free

25   and transparent elections. And in committing these crimes,

ICCQCOHs

1   Mr. Cohen has eroded faith in the electoral process and
2   compromised the rule of law. And so just as he asks for
3   leniency because of what he claims he's done for the republic,
4   the same can be true in the way in which he's undermined it.
5   All of these facts, your Honor, favor a substantial custodial
6   sentence.

7   But the second reason why a substantial custodial
8   sentence is warranted here is because of the need to promote
9   deterrence. And when it comes to Mr. Cohen, his training and
10 experience as an attorney should have been a deterrent to his
11 own criminal conduct. Instead, he used his legal license in
12 furtherance of his crimes, and that is a significant point that
13 should be taken into consideration in sentencing. A
14 substantial sentence would serve as a deterrent to future
15 criminal conduct by this particular defendant.

16   But more importantly, your Honor, a substantial
17 sentence would also serve as a general deterrent to future
18 criminal conduct by individuals like Mr. Cohen. This is
19 particularly important in the context of tax evasion and the
20 campaign's finance crimes, crimes that are difficult to detect,
21 that are so frequently orchestrated through private
22 transactions kept secret from the public. The unfairness here
23 is not to Mr. Cohen. It's to the public. Particularly in
24 light of the public interest in this case, a meaningful
25 sentence of imprisonment, one that sends a message, an

ICCQCOHs

1 appropriate message about the seriousness of these crimes is

2 appropriate. That sort of message must be sent in this case,

3 that even powerful and privileged individuals cannot violate

4 these laws with impunity.

5   Unless the Court has any questions for the government,

6 we otherwise rest on our submission

7   THE COURT: Thank you, Mr. Roos.

8   MR. PETRILLO: Just a point of clarification, your

9 Honor, if I may.

10   THE COURT: Yes. Go ahead, Mr. Petrillo.

11   MR. PETRILLO: I just want to be clear because I

12 wasn't sure whether Mr. Roos affirmed or failed to affirm that

13 the government; that is, the Southern District, by a letter

14 dated November 29 in this case captioned with this case number

15 that is the first plea before your Honor, agreed that the

16 defendant's provision of information to the Special Counsel is

17 a factor to be considered by the Court under Title 18

18 U.S. Code, Section 3553(a) in the first case, not just the

19 second case. And I wasn't sure whether I heard properly that

20 Mr. Roos was delineating between the two cases. I may just

21 have misheard, but I want to make sure it's clear.

22   MR. ROOS: Your Honor, if I may?

23   THE COURT: You may.

24   MR. ROOS: I believe this was the first point I

25 addressed, but to clarify any confusion, the government's view

ICCQCOHs

1 is that the defendant provided information that was valuable to

2 the Special Counsel's Office. We don't dispute that. And

3 that's the reason why the government is seeking or recommends a

4 modest variance in this case as opposed to seeking a guideline

5 sentence. So I guess the answer to Mr. Petrillo's question is

6 yes.

7 　　　　THE COURT: All right. Thank you.

8 　　　　Mr. Petrillo, does your client wish to address the

9 Court before sentence is imposed?

10 　　　　MR. PETRILLO: He does, your Honor, and he's asked me

11 just to clarify because he heard -- and, again, I may have

12 heard it incorrectly, that -- the amount of restitution in this

13 case; that is, the amount due and owing to the IRS is

14 approximately $1.393 million, and he's under the impression the

15 Court may have said that the guidelines range started where it

16 did because the loss amount was one and a half million. And he

17 just wanted to make sure that that point was entered into the

18 record. It doesn't change our position on the guidelines

19 though, and I am only noting it for the record.

20 　　　　And Mr. Cohen would like to be heard, your Honor.

21 　　　　THE COURT: Fine. I'll hear from Mr. Cohen now.

22 　　　　THE DEFENDANT: Your Honor, stand here or to the

23 podium?

24 　　　　THE COURT: I think it would be best to take the

25 podium.

ICCQCOHs

1   THE DEFENDANT: Thank you, your Honor.

2   I stand before your Honor humbly and painfully aware

3   that we are here today for one reason: Because of my actions

4   that I pled guilty to on August 21, and as well on November 29.

5   I take full responsibility for each act that I pled

6   guilty to, the personal ones to me and those involving the

7   President of the United States of America. Viktor Frankl in

8   his book, "Man's Search for Meaning," he wrote, "There are

9   forces beyond your control that can take away everything you

10   possess except one thing, your freedom to choose how you will

11   respond to the situation."

12   Your Honor, this may seem hard to believe, but today

13   is one of the most meaningful days of my life. The irony is

14   today is the day I am getting my freedom back as you sit at the

15   bench and you contemplate my fate.

16   I have been living in a personal and mental

17   incarceration ever since the fateful day that I accepted the

18   offer to work for a famous real estate mogul whose business

19   acumen I truly admired. In fact, I now know that there is

20   little to be admired. I want to be clear. I blame myself for

21   the conduct which has brought me here today, and it was my own

22   weakness, and a blind loyalty to this man that led me to choose

23   a path of darkness over light. It is for these reasons I chose

24   to participate in the elicit act of the President rather than

25   to listen to my own inner voice which should have warned me

ICCQCOHs

1 that the campaign finance violations that I later pled guilty

2 to were insidious.

3   Recently, the President Tweeted a statement calling me

4 weak, and he was correct, but for a much different reason than

5 he was implying. It was because time and time again I felt it

6 was my duty to cover up his dirty deeds rather than to listen

7 to my own inner voice and my moral compass. My weakness can be

8 characterized as a blind loyalty to Donald Trump, and I was

9 weak for not having the strength to question and to refuse his

10 demands. I have already spent years living a personal and

11 mental incarceration, which no matter what is decided today,

12 owning this mistake will free me to be once more the person I

13 really am.

14   Your Honor, I love my family more than anything in the

15 world: My dad who is here today, my mom, my in-laws, siblings,

16 love of my life, my wife Laura, my pride and joy, my daughter

17 Samantha, my son, Jake. There is no sentence that could

18 supersede the suffering that I live with on a daily basis,

19 knowing that my actions have brought undeserved pain and shame

20 upon my family. I deserve that pain. They do not.

21   I also stand before my children, for them to see their

22 father taking responsibility for his mistakes, mistakes that

23 have forced them to bear a shameful spotlight which they have

24 done nothing to deserve, and this breaks my heart. For me, the

25 greatest punishment has been seeing the unbearable pain that my

ICCQCOHs

1   actions and my associations have brought to my entire family.

2   My mom, my dad, this isn't what they deserve to see in their

3   older age, especially when as a child they emphasized to all of

4   us the difference between right and wrong. And I'm sorry.

5   I believed during this process that there were only

6   two things I could do to minimize the pain to my family: Admit

7   my guilt and move these proceedings along. This is why I did

8   not enter into a cooperation agreement. I have elected to be

9   sentenced without asking for adjournment. I have given

10 information during countless hours of meetings with prosecutors

11 that have been cited as substantial, meaningful and credible.

12 I have chosen this unorthodox path because the faster I am

13 sentenced, the sooner I can return to my family, be the father

14 I want to be, the husband I want to be, and a productive member

15 of society again. I do not need a cooperation agreement to be

16 in place to do the right thing. And I will continue to

17 cooperate with government, offering as much information as I

18 truthfully possess.

19   I stand behind my statement that I made to George

20 Stephanopoulos, that my wife, my daughter, my son have my first

21 loyalty and always will. I put family and country first. My

22 departure as a loyal soldier to the President bears a very

23 hefty price.

24   For months now the President of the United States, one

25 of the most powerful men in the world, publicly mocks me,

ICCQCOHs

1 calling me a rat and a liar, and insists that the Court
2 sentence me to the absolute maximum time in prison. Not only
3 is this improper; it creates a false sense that the President
4 can weigh in on the outcome of judicial proceedings that
5 implicate him. Despite being vilified by the press and
6 inundated with character assassinations over the past almost
7 two years, I still stand today, and I am committed to proving
8 my integrity and ensuring that history will not remember me as
9 the villain of his story. I now know that every action I take
10 in the future has to be well thought out and with honorable
11 intention because I wish to leave no room for future mistakes
12 in my life.
13   And so I beseech your Honor to consider this path that
14 I am currently taking when sentencing me today. And I want to
15 apologize to my entire family for what my actions have put them
16 through. My family has suffered immeasurably in the home and
17 the world outside. I know I have let them all down, and it
18 will be my life's work to make it right, and to become the best
19 version of myself.
20   Most all, I want to apologize to the people of the
21 United States. You deserve to know the truth and lying to you
22 was unjust. I want to thank you, your Honor, for all the time
23 I'm sure you've committed to this matter and the consideration
24 that you have given to my future.
25   Again, I want to thank my family, my friends, many who

ICCQCOHs

1   are here today, who are with me, especially all the people who

2   wrote letters on my behalf. In addition, I would like to thank

3   the tens of thousands of strangers who despite not knowing me

4   at all, not knowing me personally have shown kindness and

5   empathy in writing letters to me and offering support and

6   prayer. And I thank you, your Honor, I am truly sorry, and I

7   promise I will be better.

8   THE COURT: You may be seated, Mr. Cohen.

9   THE DEFENDANT: Thank you.

10   THE COURT: The defendant, Michael Cohen, comes before

11   this Court, having pled guilty to five counts of income tax

12   evasion, one count of making false statements to a banking

13   institution, one count of causing an unlawful corporate

14   contribution, and one count of an excessive campaign

15   contribution in the 18 CR 602 criminal case, and one count of

16   making false statements to the U.S. Congress in 18 CR 850.

17   Each of these crimes is a serious offense against the United

18   States.

19   Now, I've reviewed the revised presentence

20   investigation report, and I adopt the findings of fact in that

21   report as my own. I will cause the report to be docketed and

22   filed under seal as part of the record in each of these cases.

23   I have also reviewed all of the memoranda submitted by counsel

24   for the parties and the letters submitted on Mr. Cohen's

25   behalf.

ICCQCOHs

1   I previously reviewed the guidelines with all of you.

2   Suffice it to say at this juncture that with respect to the

3   first case, the guidelines range is 51 to 63 months of

4   imprisonment, and the guideline range on the second case is

5   zero to six months of imprisonment. Of course, the Sentencing

6   Guidelines should be the starting point and the initial

7   benchmark.

8   Turning to the 3553(a) factors, the question for this

9   Court is what is the appropriate and just sentence for these

10   crimes and this defendant. Mr. Cohen pled guilty to a

11   veritable smorgasbord of fraudulent conduct: Willful tax

12   evasion, making false statements to a financial institution,

13   illegal campaign contributions, and making false statements to

14   Congress. Each of the crimes involved deception and each

15   appears to have been motivated by personal greed and ambition.

16   His extensive criminal conduct also has broader public

17   consequences. Mr. Cohen evaded more than $1.3 million in

18   personal income taxes for the tax years 2012 through 2016. He

19   willfully failed to report $4 million earned through various

20   streams of income from leasing taxi medallions to consulting

21   fees and brokerage commissions. As Justice Oliver Wendell

22   Holmes famously said, "Taxes are the price we pay for a

23   civilized society."

24   Now, Mr. Cohen also made a series of false statements

25   to financial institutions regarding his liabilities and monthly

1 expenses so that he would be approved for a $500,000 home

2 equity line of credit.

3   Further, Mr. Cohen committed two campaign finance

4 crimes on the eve of the 2016 presidential election with the

5 intent to influence the outcome of that election. He made or

6 facilitated payments to silence two women who threatened to go

7 public with details of purported extramarital affairs, and

8 Mr. Cohen admitted that he did so in coordination with and at

9 the direction of Individual One.

10   Finally, in a separate criminal proceeding filed by

11 the Special Counsel's Office, Mr. Cohen admitted that he made

12 false statements about a proposed business project in Moscow to

13 congressional committees investigating possible interference by

14 the Russian government with the 2016 presidential election.

15 Each of these crimes standing alone warrant serious punishment.

16   The financial harms are readily ascertainable.

17 Mr. Cohen's tax evasion offenses cheated the federal government

18 out of $1,393,858. His deception caused a bank to approve a

19 $500,000 line of credit he did not deserve. And even his

20 campaign finance crimes may be measured by the amount of

21 unlawful contributions: The $150,000 hush money payment that

22 he coordinated, and the $130,000 hush money payment that he

23 funneled from his home equity loan through a shell corporation.

24   While this is his first conviction, the magnitude,

25 breadth, and duration of his criminal conduct requires specific

ICCQCOHs

1   deterrence. Tax and campaign finance prosecutions are rare,

2   but unlike the mine-run tax evasion or campaign finance

3   violation, Mr. Cohen's crimes implicate a far more insidious

4   harm to our democratic institutions, especially in view of his

5   subsequent plea to making false statements to Congress. Thus,

6   the need for general deterrence is amplified in this case.

7   Now, Mr. Cohen had a comfortable childhood and enjoyed

8   all the privileges of growing up in a close-knit, upper class

9   suburb on Long Island. He and his siblings had loving parents

10 who worked hard to provide everything for their children. He

11 graduated from law school and practiced law in various law

12 firms until the Trump organization hired him as an attorney in

13 2007. Thereafter, his entire professional life apparently

14 revolved around the Trump organization. He thrived on his

15 access to wealthy and powerful people, and he became one

16 himself.

17   The letters submitted on his behalf reveal a man

18 dedicated to his family and generous with his time and money to

19 help people in his own orbit. A number of individuals have

20 written to me describing how Mr. Cohen came to their aid

21 without seeking anything in return. Of course, that kind of

22 generosity is laudable. But somewhere along the way Mr. Cohen

23 appears to have lost his moral compass and sought instead to

24 monetize his new-found influence. That trajectory,

25 unfortunately, has led him to this courtroom today.

ICCQCOHs

1   While Mr. Cohen does not have a formal cooperation

2   agreement with the United States Attorney's Office, he has

3   nevertheless met with prosecutors on a number of occasions.

4   The Special Counsel's Office notes that he has voluntarily

5   provided information "about his own conduct and that of others

6   on core topics under investigation" by the Special Counsel and

7   that the information he has provided has been "relevant and

8   useful."Further, the Special Counsel urges that any sentence

9   imposed in connection with 18 CR 850 should be concurrent to

10   any sentence imposed in the earlier case.

11   While the United States Attorney's Office acknowledges

12   that Mr. Cohen's assistance to the Special Counsel's Office was

13   "significant" and warrants a modest variance from the

14   guidelines range, they contend that it should not approach the

15   type of credit typically given to cooperating witnesses in this

16   district.

17   However, cooperation, even when it is not the product

18   of a formal agreement, should be encouraged where information

19   is provided that advances criminal investigations. Our system

20   of justice would be less robust without the use of cooperating

21   witnesses to assist law enforcement.

22   Based on the submissions of the parties, this Court

23   agrees that Mr. Cohen should receive some credit for providing

24   assistance to the Special Counsel's Office. While Mr. Cohen

25   pledges to assist the Special Counsel's Office in further

1   investigations, that is not a matter that this Court can

2   consider now.

3   There is an acute need for the sentence here to

4   reflect the seriousness of the offenses and to promote respect

5   for the law. As a lawyer, Mr. Cohen should have known better.

6   Tax evasion undercuts the government's ability to provide

7   essential services on which we all depend. False statements to

8   banking institutions undermine the integrity of our financial

9   system. Campaign finance violations threaten the fairness of

10 elections, and false statements to Congress interfere with the

11 fact-finding process in matters of national importance.

12   While Mr. Cohen has taken steps to mitigate his

13 criminal conduct by pleading guilty and volunteering useful

14 information to prosecutors, that does not wipe the slate clean.

15 Mr. Cohen selected the information he disclosed to the

16 government. This Court cannot agree with the defendant's

17 assertion that no jail time is warranted. In fact, this Court

18 firmly believes that a significant term of imprisonment is

19 fully justified in this highly publicized case to send a

20 message to those who contemplate avoiding their taxes, evading

21 campaign finance laws or lying to financial institutions or

22 Congress. Our democratic institutions depend on the honesty of

23 our citizenry in dealing with the government. And so it is

24 against that backdrop that I am prepared to sentence the

25 defendant.

ICCQCOHs

1   Mr. Cohen I'd ask, sir, that you stand at this time.

2   Mr. Cohen, it's my judgment, sir, that on 18 CR 602

3   that you be sentenced to a term of 36 months of imprisonment to

4   be followed by three years of supervised release on each count

5   to be served concurrently with the sentence that I will impose

6   in a moment on 18 CR 850. I'm imposing all of the standard

7   conditions of supervised release and the following special

8   condition: That you provide the probation department with

9   access to any requested financial information.

10   Further, I'm going to enter an order of forfeiture in

11   this case in the amount of $500,000, and I'm going to enter an

12   order for restitution in the amount of $1,393,858. I am also

13   going to impose a fine of $50,000, and the mandatory special

14   assessment of $800.

15   Now, with respect to 18 CR 850, I sentence you to two

16   months of imprisonment to be served concurrently with the term

17   imposed in 18 CR 602 to be followed by three years of

18   supervised release, also to be served concurrently with the

19   term imposed in 18 CR 602, and with all of the standard

20   conditions of supervised release.

21   In this case with respect to 18 CR 850, I am also

22   going to impose a $50,000 fine in that case to recognize the

23   gravity of the harm of lying to Congress in matters of national

24   importance. And, once again, I will impose the mandatory

25   special assessment in that case of $100.

ICCQCOHs

1   Just to be clear, the sentence in the earlier case is

2 concurrent on all counts in that information.

3   And so, Mr. Cohen, this constitutes the sentence of

4 this Court. I advise you that to the extent you have not

5 previously waived your right to appeal, you have the right to

6 appeal. I advise you further that if you cannot afford

7 counsel, counsel will be provided to you free of cost.

8 Mr. Petrillo has done a superb job in navigating you through

9 this matter and bringing the sentencing submissions before the

10 Court. I'm confident that he and Ms. Lester will advise you

11 further with respect to your appellate rights. You may be

12 seated, sir.

13   Are there any further applications at this time?

14   MR. ROOS: Not from the government, your Honor.

15   THE COURT: Ms. Rhee.

16   MS. RHEE: Your Honor, the Special Counsel's Office

17 would just like to confirm that there will be a separate

18 $50,000 fine.

19   THE COURT: Yes.

20   MS. RHEE: Not to run concurrently.

21   THE COURT: No, it's a separate fine. It's a separate

22 harm, and the guidelines in my view do not recognize the

23 gravity of the offense of making false statements to Congress.

24   MS. RHEE: Thank you for the clarification.

25   THE COURT: Mr. Petrillo.

ICCQCOHs

1   MR. PETRILLO: Your Honor, if you would, would the

2   Court give consideration to voluntary surrender by the

3   defendant and consider recommending the designation of

4   Otisville as the place of imprisonment?

5   THE COURT: I will make that recommendation, and I

6   will allow for a voluntary surrender in this case. What

7   surrender date are you seeking?

8   MR. PETRILLO: I don't have one particularly in mind,

9   but from past experience it seems to take about 10 or 12 weeks

10 for the BOP to --

11   THE COURT: Right. Is March 6 all right? And if for

12 some reason you've not been notified of a designated

13 institution, just write a short note to me, and I will put the

14 surrender date over.

15   MR. PETRILLO: Very well.

16   THE COURT: Go ahead.

17   MR. PETRILLO: I have one other thing for the record

18 that doesn't require a ruling, but as you know, under *United*

19 *States v. Ganais* in the Second Circuit, it's incumbent upon the

20 defendant to demand his property back post a search procedure

21 as part of protecting his rights under the Fourth Amendment.

22 And so for the record, I'd like to make that demand and thus

23 have no confusion as to where that stands.

24   THE COURT: All right. I'm confident there will be

25 further briefing with respect to that matter after this

ICCQCOHs

1   proceeding is concluded, and I will await receipt of some

2   submission.

3   This matter is concluded. Have a good afternoon

4   (Adjourned)

5

6

7

8

9

10

11

12

13

14

15

16

17

18

19

20

21

22

23

24

25

THE CONGRESSIONAL TESTIMONY

FEBRUARY 27, 2019

Meeting on: Michael Cohen, Former Attorney to President Donald Trump

Date: 2-27-19
Convened: 10:01 a.m.

Recesses: 12:10 p.m. - 12:22 p.m. and 2:34 p.m. – 4:27 p.m.

Adjourned: 5:20 p.m.

Democrats	Present	Time	Republicans	Present	Time
MR. CUMMINGS (MD) *(Chairman)*	X		MR. JORDAN (OH) *(Ranking Member)*	X	
MS. MALONEY (NY)	X		MR. AMASH (MI)	X	
MS. NORTON (DC)	X		MR. GOSAR (AZ)	X	
MR. CLAY (MO)	X		MS. FOXX (NC)	X	
MR. LYNCH (MA)	X		MR. MASSIE (KY)	X	
MR. COOPER (TN)	X		MR. MEADOWS (NC)	X	
MR. CONNOLLY (VA)	X		MR. HICE (GA)	X	
MR. KRISHNAMOORTHI (IL)	X		MR. GROTHMAN (WI)	X	
MR. RASKIN (MD)	X		MR. COMER (KY)	X	
MR. ROUDA (CA)	X		MR. CLOUD (TX)	X	
MS. HILL (CA)	X		MR. GIBBS (OH)	X	
MS. WASSERMAN SCHULTZ (FL)	X		MR. HIGGINS (LA)	X	
MR. SARBANES (MD)	X		MR. NORMAN (SC)	X	
MR. WELCH (VT)	X		MR. ROY (TX)	X	
MS. SPEIER (CA)	X		MS. MILLER (WV)	X	
MS. KELLY (IL)	X		MR. GREEN (TN)	X	
MR. DeSAULNIER (CA)	X		MR. ARMSTRONG (ND)	X	
MS. LAWRENCE (MI)	X		MR. STEUBE (FL)	X	
MS. PLASKETT (VI)	X				
MR. KHANNA (CA)	X				
MR. GOMEZ (CA)	X				
MS. OCASIO-CORTEZ (NY)	X				
MS. PRESSLEY (MA)	X				
MS. TLAIB (MI)	X				

Ranking Member's Statement ended at 10:25 a.m.

Rep. Mark Meadows (R, North Carolina): Mr. Chairman I have a point of order.

Rep. Elijah Cummings (D, Maryland): You will state your point of order.

Meadows: Rule 9(f) of the committee rules say that any testimony from your witness needs to be here 24 hours in advance. The committee, the chairman knows well that at 10:08 we received the written testimony—and then we received evidence this morning at 7:54. Now, if this was just an oversight, Mr. Chairman, I could look beyond it. But it was an intentional effort by this witness and his advisers to once again show his disdain for this body. And with that, I move that we postpone this hearing.

Cummings: I want to thank the gentlemen. Let me say that this we got the testimony late last night. We did. And we got it to you all pretty much the same time that we got it. I want to move forward with this hearing.

Meadows: Mr. Chairman, with all due respect, Mr. Chairman, this is a violation of the rule. And—and if it was not intentional I would—I would not have a problem. I'm not saying it was intentional on your part. I'm saying it's intentional on his part, because Mr. Dean last night on a cable news network actually made it all very evident. John Dean. I'll quote, Mr. Chairman. He said, "As a former committee counsel in the house judiciary and then a long-term witness, sitting alone at the table is important." Quote: "Holding your statement as long as you can so the other side can't chew it up is important as well." Close quote. And so—so it was advice that our witness got for this particular body. And, Mr. Chairman, when you were in the minority you wouldn't have stood for it. I can tell that you we should not stand for it as a body, Mr. Chairman.

Cummings: Let me say this . . . . Yes, Katie Hill?

Rep. Katie Hill (D, California): I move to table.

Rep. Jordan (R, Ohio): Mr. Chairman. Mr. Chairman, I was asked to be recognized before the motion.

Cummings: The vote is so in tabling the motion to postpone.

Jordan: You know who had this before all the members of the committee? CNN had it before it we did. CNN had it before. I want to be recognized.

Cummings: Well, the vote is on tabling the motion to postpone. All in favor say aye, all opposed say no. The ayes have it.

Meadows: I appeal the ruling of the chair. Yes I—I can I assure you it's in the rules. I appeal the ruling of the chair.

Hill: I move to waive the rules. I move to table.

Meadows: She made two motions. What's the motion?

Cummings: The vote is on tabling.

Hill: I move to table the appeal to the ruling of the chair.

Cummings: The vote is on that. All in favor say aye. All opposed say no. The ayes have it.

Meadows: I ask for a recorded vote, Mr. Chairman.

Cummings: Very well, the clerk will call the role.

Clerk: Mr. Cummings. Mr. Cummings votes yes. Ms. Maloney. Ms. Maloney votes yes. Ms. Norton. Ms. Norton votes yes. Mr. Clay. Mr. Clay votes yes. Mr. Lynch. Mr. Lynch votes yes. Mr. Cooper. Mr. Cooper votes yes. Mr. Connolly. Mr. Connolly votes yes. Mr. Krishnamoorthi. Mr. Krishnamoorthi votes yes. Mr. Raskin. Mr. Raskin votes yes. Mr. Rouda. Mr. Rouda votes yes. Ms. Hill. Ms. Hill votes yes. Ms. Wasserman-Schultz. Ms. Wasserman-Schultz votes yes. Mr. Sarbanes. Mr. Sarbanes votes yes. Mr. Welch. Mr. Welch votes yes. Ms. Speier. Ms. Speier votes yes. Ms. Kelly. Ms. Kelly votes yes. Mr. DeSaulnier. Mr. DeSaulnier votes yes. Ms. Lawrence. Ms. Lawrence votes yes. Ms. Plaskett. Ms. Plaskett votes yes. Mr. Khanna. Mr. Khanna votes yes. Mr. Gomez. Mr. Gomez votes yes. Ms. Ocasio-Cortez. Ms. Ocasio-Cortez votes yes. Ms. Pressley. Ms. Pressley votes yes. Ms. Tlaib. Ms. Tlaib votes yes. Mr. Jordan. Mr. Jordan votes no. Mr. Amash. Mr. Amash votes no. Mr. Gosar. Mr. Gosar votes no. Ms.

Foxx. Ms. Foxx votes no. Mr. Massey. Mr. Massey votes no. Mr. Meadows. Mr. Meadows votes no. Mr. Hice. Mr. Hice votes no. Mr. Grothman. Mr. Grothman votes no. Mr. Comer. Mr. Comer votes no. Mr. Cloud. Mr. Cloud votes no. Mr. Gibbs. Mr. Gibbs votes no Mr. Higgins. Mr. Norman. Mr. Norman votes no. Mr. Roy. Mr. Roy votes no. Ms. Miller. Ms. Miller votes no. Mr. Green. Mr. Green votes no. Mr. Armstrong. Mr. Armstrong votes no. Mr. Steube. Mr. Steube votes no. On this vote we have 24 yeses, 17 nos.

Cummings: The motion to table is agreed to. The let me say this. You made it clear that did you not want the American people to hear what Mr. Cohen has to say. But the American people have a right to hear him. So we're going to proceed. The American people can judge his credibility for themselves. Now—

Jordan: Mr. Chairman.

Cummings: Yes.

Jordan: We did not say that. We said we wanted to follow the rules. We didn't say stop the hearing; just postpone it so we can get his testimony and exhibits when we were supposed to get them according to the rules of the committee. That's all we said. We didn't say we wanted to hear from the guy.

Cummings: I'm claiming my time. I recognize myself for five minutes to give an opening statement.

Good morning. Today, the Committee will hear testimony from Michael Cohen, President Donald Trump's longtime personal attorney and one of his closest and most trusted advisors over the last decade. On August 21, Mr. Cohen appeared in federal court and admitted to arranging secret payoffs of hundreds of thousands of dollars on the eve of the election to silence women alleging affairs with Donald Trump.

Mr. Cohen admitted to violating campaign finance laws and other laws. He admitted to committing these felonies quote, "in coordination with, and at the direction of" President Trump. And he admitted to lying about his actions to protect the President. Some will certainly ask, if Mr. Cohen was lying then, why should we believe him now? That is a legitimate question.

Here is how I view our role. Every one of us in this room has a duty to serve as an independent check on the Executive Branch. We are searching for the truth. The President has made many statements of his own, and now the American people have a right.

We received a copy of Mr. Cohen's written statement late last night. It includes not only personal eyewitness accounts of meetings with Donald Trump as President inside the Oval Office, but it also includes documents and other corroborating evidence for some of Mr. Cohen's statements. For example, Mr. Cohen has provided a copy of a check sent while the President was in office—with Donald Trump's signature on it—to reimburse Mr. Cohen for the hush-money payment to Stormy Daniels.

This new evidence raises a host of troubling legal and ethical concerns about the President's actions in the White

House and before. This check is dated August 1, 2017. Six months later, in April of 2018, the President denied knowing anything about it. In April 2018, President Trump was flying on Air Force One when a reporter asked him, quote: "Did you know about the $130,000 payment to Stormy Daniels?" The President answered, quote: "No."

A month after that, the President admitted making payments to Mr. Cohen, but claimed they were part of "a monthly retainer" for legal services. This claim fell apart in August when federal prosecutors concluded, quote: "In truth and in fact, there was no such retainer agreement." Today we will also hear Mr. Cohen's account of a meeting in 2016 in Donald Trump's office during which Roger Stone said, over a speakerphone, that he had just spoken with Julian Assange, who said there would be a, quote, "massive dump of emails that would damage Hillary Clinton's campaign."

According to Mr. Cohen, Mr. Trump replied, "Wouldn't that be great." The testimony that Michael Cohen will provide today is deeply disturbing. We will all have to make our own evaluation of the evidence and Mr. Cohen's credibility. As he admits, he has repeatedly lied in the past. I agree with Ranking Member Jordan that this is an important factor we all need to weigh. 8 But where I disagree fundamentally with the Ranking Member involves his efforts to prevent the American people from hearing from Mr. Cohen. Mr. Cohen's testimony raises grave questions about the legality of the Donald Trump's conduct and the truthfulness of his statements while he was President. We need to assess and investigate this new evidence as we uphold our constitutional oversight responsibilities. And we will continue after today to gather more documents and testimony in our search for the truth.

The American people voted for accountability in November, and they have a right to hear Mr. Cohen in public so they can make their own judgments. Mr. Cohen's testimony is the beginning of the process—not the end. The days of this Committee protecting the President at all costs are over. Before I close, I want to comment about the scope of today's hearing.

At the request of the House Intelligence Committee, I had intended—over the objections of the Ranking Member—to limit the scope of today's hearing to avoid questions about Russia. However, in Mr. Cohen's written testimony, he has made statements relating to Russia, and these are topics that we understand do not raise concern from the Department of Justice. So in fairness to the Ranking Member and all Committee members, we will not restrict questions relating to the witness' testimony or related questions he is willing to answer.

Finally, I remind members that we still need to remain mindful of those areas where there are ongoing interests of the Department of Justice. Those scoping limitations have not been changed. Finally, and to Mr. Cohen, Martin Luther King, Mr. Cohen, said some words I leave with you today before you testify. He said, "Faith is taking the first step, even when you can't see the whole staircase. There comes a time when silence becomes betrayal. Our lives begin to end the day we become silent about things that truly matter. In the end," he says, "we will remember not the words of our enemies but the silence of our friends." And with that, I yield to the distinguished gentleman, the ranking member of our committee, Mr. Jordan.

Mr. Jordan is recognized for his opening statement.

Jordan: Mr. Chairman, here we go. Here we go. For your first big hearing, your first announced witness, Michael Cohen. I want everyone in this room the first announced witness for the 116th Congress is a guy going to prison in two months for lying to Congress. Mr. Chairman, your chairmanship will always be identified with this hearing. And we all need to understand what this is. This is the Michael Cohen hearing presented by Lanny Davis. That's right. Lanny Davis choreographed the whole thing. The Clintons' best friend, the loyalist operative Lanny Davis. You know how we know? He told our staff. He told the committee staff. He said the hearing was his idea, he had to talk Michael Cohen into coming, and he had to persuade the chairman to have it. He told us it took two months to get the job done. But here we are. He talked him into it.

This might be the first time someone convicted of lying to Congress has appeared again so quickly in front of Congress. Certainly it's the first time a convicted perjurer has been brought back to be a star witness in a hearing. And there is a reason this is a first. Because no other committee would do it. Think about this. With Mr. Cohen here, this committee—we got lots of lawyers on this committee—this committee is actually encouraging a witness to violate attorney-client privilege. Mr. Chairman, when we delegitimize dishonesty, we delegitimize this institution. You have stacked the deck against the truth. We're only allowed to ask certain questions even with the amendment you told us about, Russia is on the table. You initially told us you we can't ask questions about the special counsel, the Southern District of New York. Can't ask questions about Russia.

Nope, nope, the only subjects we can talk about are ones you think are going to be harmful to the President of the United States. And the answers to those questions are going to come from a guy who can't be trusted.

Here is what the U.S. attorney said about Mr. Cohen: "While Mr. Cohen enjoyed a privileged life, his desire for forever greater wealth and influence precipitated an intensive course of criminal conduct. Mr. Cohen committed four distinct federal crimes over a period of several years, he was motivated to do so by personal greed and repeatedly—repeatedly—used his power and influence for deceptive ends."

But the Democrats don't care. They don't care. They just want to use you, Mr. Cohen. You're their patsy today. They got to find somebody, somewhere, to say something so they can try to remove the President from office. Because Tom Steyer told them to. Tom Steyer last week organized the town hall, guess where? Chairman Nadler's district in Manhattan. Two nights ago Tom Steyer organized a town hall, guess where? Chairman Cumming's district in Baltimore. The best they can find, the best they can find to start this process, Michael Cohen. Fraudster, cheat, convicted felon, in two months a federal inmate. Actually they didn't find him; Lanny Davis did.

I'll say one thing about the Democrats: They stick to the playbook. Remember how all this started: The Clinton campaign hired Perkins Coie law firm, who hired Glenn Simpson, who hired Christopher Steele, who put together the fake dossier that the FBI used to get a warrant to spy on the Trump campaign. When that whole scheme failed and the American people said we're making Donald Trump President, they said we got to do something else. So now Clinton loyalist, Clinton operative Lanny Davis persuaded the chairman of the oversight committee to give a convicted felon a forum to tell stories and lie about the President of the United States. So they can all start their impeachment process.

Mr. Chairman, we are better than this. We are better than this. I yield back.

Cummings: I wanted to note . . . .

Jordan: Mr. Chairman, I have a motion. I have a motion under rule 2(k)(6).

Cummings: You yielded back, sir. You yielded back.

Jordan: Mr. Chairman, you took seven minutes; I took four.

Cummings: Well the gentleman yielded back.

Jordan: That's how you operate? First you don't follow the rules and now you're going to say you don't get—you get to . . . .

Cummings: Point of order.

Jordan: You get to deviate from the rules?

Cummings: Regular order.

Jordan: I just have a simple motion, Mr. Chairman. It's a point of order to have the testimony 24 hours in advance.

Cummings: Excuse me. I wanted to note that under rule 11, all media and photographers must be officially credentialed to record these proceedings and take photographs. I also wanted to briefly address the spectators in the hearing room today. We welcome you and we respect your right to be here. We also ask in turn for your respect as we proceed with the business of the committee today. It is the intention of the committee to proceed without any disruptions. Any disruptions of this committee will result in the United States capitol police restoring order and protesters will be removed. And we are grateful for your presence here today and your cooperation. Now I want to welcome Mr. Cohen and thank him for participating in today's hearing. Mr. Cohen, if you would please rice and I will begin to swear you in. Raise your right hand. Do you swear or affirm that the testimony that you are about to give is the whole truth, and nothing but the truth, so help you God? Let the record show the witness answered in the affirmative. Thank you. You may be seated. The microphones are sensitive to please speak directly into them. Without objection your written statement will be made part of the record. With that, Mr. Cohen, you are recognized to give an oral presentation of your testimony. Is your mic on?

Cohen: Yes. Chairman Cummings, Ranking Member Jordan, and Members of the Committee, thank you for inviting me here today. I have asked this Committee to ensure that my family be protected from Presidential threats, and that the Committee be sensitive to the questions pertaining to ongoing investigations. Thank you for your help and for your understanding. I am here under oath to correct the record, to answer the Committee's questions truthfully, and to offer the American people what I know about President Trump.

I recognize that some of you may doubt and attack me on my credibility. It is for this reason that I have incorporated into this opening statement documents that are irrefutable, and demonstrate that the information you will hear is accurate and truthful.

Never in a million years did I imagine, when I accepted a job in 2007 to work for Donald Trump, that he would one day run for President, launch a campaign on a platform of hate and intolerance, and actually win. I regret the day I said "yes" to Mr. Trump. I regret all the help and support I gave him along the way.

I am ashamed of my own failings, and I publicly accepted responsibility for them by pleading guilty in the Southern District of New York. I am ashamed of my weakness and misplaced loyalty—of the things I did for Mr. Trump in an effort to protect and promote him. I am ashamed that I chose to take part in concealing Mr. Trump's illicit acts rather than listening to my own conscience.

I am ashamed because I know what Mr. Trump is.

He is a racist.

He is a conman.

He is a cheat.

He was a presidential candidate who knew that Roger Stone was talking with Julian Assange about a WikiLeaks drop of Democratic National Committee emails.

I will explain each in a few moments.

I am providing the Committee today with several documents. These include:

- A copy of a check Mr. Trump wrote from his personal bank account—after he became president—to reimburse me for the hush money payments I made to cover up his affair with an adult film star and prevent damage to his campaign;

- Copies of financial statements for 2011–2013 that he gave to such institutions as Deutsche Bank;
- A copy of an article with Mr. Trump's handwriting on it that reported on the auction of a portrait of himself— he arranged for the bidder ahead of time and then re- imbursed the bidder from the account of his non-profit charitable foundation, with the picture now hanging in one of his country clubs; and
- Copies of letters I wrote at Mr. Trump's direction that threatened his high school, colleges, and the College Board not to release his grades or SAT scores.

I hope my appearance here today, my guilty plea, and my work with law enforcement agencies are steps along a path of redemption that will restore faith in me and help this country understand our president better.

Before going further, I want to apologize to each of you and to Congress as a whole.

The last time I appeared before Congress, I came to pro- tect Mr. Trump. Today, I'm here to tell the truth about Mr. Trump.

I lied to Congress about when Mr. Trump stopped nego- tiating the Moscow Tower project in Russia. I stated that we stopped negotiating in January 2016. That was false: Our ne- gotiations continued for months later during the campaign.

Mr. Trump did not directly tell me to lie to Congress. That's not how he operates. In conversations we had during the campaign, at the same time I was actively negotiating in Russia for him, he would look me in the eye and tell me there's no business in Russia and then go out and lie to the American people by saying the same thing. In his way, he was telling me to lie. There were at least a half-dozen times between the Iowa Caucus in January 2016 and the end of June when he would ask me "How's it going in Russia?"—referring to the Moscow Tower project. You need to know that Mr. Trump's personal lawyers reviewed and edited my statement to Congress about the timing of the Moscow Tower negotiations before I gave it.

To be clear: Mr. Trump knew of and directed the Trump Moscow negotiations throughout the campaign and lied about it. He lied about it because he never expected to win the election. He also lied about it because he stood to make hundreds of millions of dollars on the Moscow real estate project.

And so I lied about it, too—because Mr. Trump had made clear to me, through his personal statements to me that we both knew were false and through his lies to the country, that he wanted me to lie. And he made it clear to me because his personal attorneys reviewed my statement before I gave it to Congress.

Over the past two years, I have been smeared as "a rat" by the President of the United States. The truth is much different, and let me take a brief moment to introduce myself.

My name is Michael Dean Cohen.

I am a blessed husband of 24 years and a father to an incredible daughter and son. When I married my wife, I promised her that I would love her, cherish her, and protect her. As my father said countless times throughout my childhood, "you my wife, and you my children, are the air that I breathe." To my Laura, my Sami, and my Jake, there is nothing I wouldn't do to protect you.

I have always tried to live a life of loyalty, friendship, generosity, and compassion—qualities my parents ingrained in my siblings and me since childhood. My father survived the

Holocaust thanks to the compassion and selfless acts of others. He was helped by many who put themselves in harm's way to do what they knew was right.

That is why my first instinct has always been to help those in need. Mom and Dad . . . I am sorry that I let you down.

As many people that know me best would say, I am the person they would call at 3am if they needed help. I proudly remember being the emergency contact for many of my children's friends when they were growing up because their parents knew that I would drop everything and care for them as if they were my own.

Yet, last fall I pled guilty in federal court to felonies for the benefit of, at the direction of, and in coordination with Individual #1.

For the record: Individual #1 is President Donald J. Trump.

It is painful to admit that I was motivated by ambition at times. It is even more painful to admit that many times I ignored my conscience and acted loyal to a man when I should not have. Sitting here today, it seems unbelievable that I was so mesmerized by Donald Trump that I was willing to do things for him that I knew were absolutely wrong.

For that reason, I have come here to apologize to my family, to the government, and to the American people.

Accordingly, let me now tell you about Mr. Trump. I got to know him very well, working very closely with him for more than 10 years, as his Executive Vice President and Special Counsel and then personal attorney when he became President. When I first met Mr. Trump, he was a successful entrepreneur, a real estate giant, and an icon. Being around Mr. Trump was intoxicating. When you were in his presence, you felt like you were involved in something greater than yourself—that you were somehow changing the world.

I wound up touting the Trump narrative for over a decade. That was my job. Always stay on message. Always defend. It monopolized my life. At first, I worked mostly on real estate developments and other business transactions. Shortly thereafter, Mr. Trump brought me into his personal life and private dealings. Over time, I saw his true character revealed.

Mr. Trump is an enigma. He is complicated, as am I. He has both good and bad, as do we all. But the bad far outweighs the good, and since taking office, he has become the worst version of himself. He is capable of behaving kindly, but he is not kind. He is capable of committing acts of generosity, but he is not generous. He is capable of being loyal, but he is fundamentally disloyal.

Donald Trump is a man who ran for office to make his brand great, not to make our country great. He had no desire or intention to lead this nation—only to market himself and to build his wealth and power. Mr. Trump would often say, this campaign was going to be the "greatest infomercial in political history."

He never expected to win the primary. He never expected to win the general election. The campaign—for him—was always a marketing opportunity.

I knew early on in my work for Mr. Trump that he would direct me to lie to further his business interests. I am ashamed to say, that when it was for a real estate mogul in the private sector, I considered it trivial. As the President, I consider it significant and dangerous. But in the mix, lying for Mr. Trump was normalized, and no one around him questioned it. In fairness, no one around him today questions it, either.

A lot of people have asked me about whether Mr. Trump knew about the release of the hacked Democratic National Committee emails ahead of time. The answer is yes. As I earlier stated, Mr. Trump knew from Roger Stone in advance about the WikiLeaks drop of emails. In July 2016, days before the Democratic convention, I was in Mr. Trump's office when his secretary announced that Roger Stone was on the phone. Mr. Trump put Mr. Stone on the speakerphone. Mr. Stone told Mr. Trump that he had just gotten off the phone with Julian Assange and that Mr. Assange told Mr. Stone that, within a couple of days, there would be a massive dump of emails that would damage Hillary Clinton's campaign. Mr. Trump responded by stating to the effect of "wouldn't that be great."

Mr. Trump is a racist.

The country has seen Mr. Trump court white supremacists and bigots. You have heard him call poorer countries "shitholes." In private, he is even worse. He once asked me if I could name a country run by a black person that wasn't a "shithole." This was when Barack Obama was President of the United States. While we were once driving through a struggling neighborhood in Chicago, he commented that only black people could live that way. And, he told me that black people would never vote for him because they were too stupid.

And yet I continued to work for him.

Mr. Trump is a cheat.

As previously stated, I'm giving the Committee today three years of President Trump's financial statements, from 2011-2013, which he gave to Deutsche Bank to inquire about a loan to buy the Buffalo Bills and to Forbes. These are Exhibits 1a, 1b, and 1c to my testimony.

DONALD J. TRUMP

STATEMENT OF FINANCIAL CONDITION

JUNE 30, 2011

(See Independent Accountants' Compilation Report)

ASSETS

Cash and marketable securities	$ 258,900,000
Escrow and reserve deposits and prepaid expenses	9,100,000
Real and operating properties:	
Trump Tower - 725 Fifth Avenue, New York, New York	490,000,000
NIKETOWN - East 57th Street, New York, New York	263,700,000
40 Wall Street - New York, New York	524,700,000
Trump Park Avenue - New York, New York	311,600,000
Club facilities and related real estate - New York, Florida, New Jersey, California, Washington DC and Scotland	1,314,600,000
The Trump World Tower at United Nations Plaza - New York, New York	21,400,000
100 Central Park South - New York, New York	31,300,000
Trump Plaza, commercial and retained residential portions - New York, New York	28,200,000
Trump Palace, Trump Parc and Trump Parc East Condominiums, commercial portions - New York, New York	12,900,000
Trump International Hotel and Tower - New York, New York	27,400,000
Properties under development - Westchester County, New York and Beverly Hills, California	273,200,000
Partnerships and joint ventures - (net of related debt):	
1290 Sixth Avenue, New York, New York and 555 California Street, San Francisco, California	720,900,000
Miss Universe Pageants	15,000,000
Real estate licensing developments	110,000,000
Other assets	184,100,000
Total assets	$ 4,597,000,000

The accompanying notes are an integral part of this financial statement.

Exhibit 1a

LIABILITIES AND NET WORTH

Accounts payable, accrued expenses and retention payable	$	3,700,000
Loans payable on real and operating properties:		
Loan related to Trump Tower		27,770,000
Secured lease bonds – NIKETOWN		53,080,000
Loan related to 40 Wall Street		160,000,000
Loans related to club facilities and related real estate		24,170,000
Loan related to Trump Park Avenue		22,750,000
Loan related to the commercial and retained residential portions of Trump Plaza		8,470,000
Loan related to Trump International Hotel and Tower, New York		7,000,000
Loan related to properties under development in Westchester County, New York		7,690,000
Mortgages and loans payable secured by other assets		20,780,000
		335,410,000
Commitments and contingencies		
Net worth		4,261,590,000
Total liabilities and net worth	$	4,597,000,000

3

Exhibit 1a (cont.)

DONALD J. TRUMP

STATEMENT OF FINANCIAL CONDITION

JUNE 30, 2012

(See Independent Accountants' Compilation Report)

ASSETS

Cash and marketable securities	$ 169,700,000
Escrow and reserve deposits and prepaid expenses	10,780,000
Real and operating properties:	
Trump Tower - 725 Fifth Avenue, New York, New York	501,100,000
NIKETOWN - East 57th Street, New York, New York	279,500,000
40 Wall Street - New York, New York	527,200,000
Trump Park Avenue - New York, New York	312,400,000
Club facilities and related real estate - New York, Florida, New Jersey, California, Washington DC, North Carolina and Scotland	1,570,300,000
The Trump World Tower at United Nations Plaza - New York, New York	18,200,000
100 Central Park South - New York, New York	32,700,000
Trump Plaza, commercial and retained residential portions - New York, New York	30,100,000
Trump Palace, Trump Parc and Trump Parc East Condominiums, commercial portions - New York, New York	13,000,000
Trump International Hotel and Tower - New York, New York	27,600,000
Mansion at Seven Springs - Bedford, New York	291,000,000
Partnerships and joint ventures - (net of related debt):	
1290 Avenue of the Americas, New York, New York and 555 California Street, San Francisco, California	823,300,000
Miss Universe Pageants	15,000,000
Real estate licensing developments	85,000,000
Other assets	303,500,000
Total assets	$ 5,010,380,000

The accompanying notes are an integral part of this financial statement.

Exhibit 1b

LIABILITIES AND NET WORTH

Accounts payable and accrued expenses	$	4,400,000
Loans payable on real and operating properties:		
Loan related to Trump Tower		26,890,000
Secured lease bonds – NIKETOWN		46,390,000
Loan related to 40 Wall Street		160,000,000
Loans related to club facilities and related real estate		148,360,000
Loan related to Trump Park Avenue		22,190,000
Loan related to the commercial and retained residential portions of Trump Plaza		8,300,000
Loan related to Trump International Hotel and Tower, New York		7,000,000
Loan related to Mansion at Seven Springs		7,520,000
Mortgages and loans payable secured by other assets		20,650,000
		451,700,000
Commitments and contingencies		
Net worth		4,558,680,000
Total liabilities and net worth	$	5,010,380,000

3

Donald J. Trump
Summary of Net Worth
As of March 31, 2013

ASSETS

Cash & Marketable Securities - as reflected herein is **after** the acquisition of numerous assets (i.e. multiple aircraft, land, golf courses, etc), the paying off of significant mortgages for cash and before the collection of significant receivables.	346,100,000	
Escrow and reserve deposits and prepaid expenses	10,780,000	
Real & Operating Properties owned 100% by Donald J. Trump through various entities controlled by him:		
Commercial Properties (New York City)	1,381,350,000	
Residential Properties (New York City)	351,550,000	
Club facilities & related real estate	1,570,300,000	
Property under Development	291,000,000	
Real Properties owned less than 100% by Donald J. Trump 1290 Avenue of the Americas - New York City Bank of America Building - San Francisco, California		
Total Value Net of Debt	823,300,000	
Real Estate Licensing Deals	74,140,000	
Miss Universe, Miss USA and Miss Teen USA Pageants	15,000,000	
Other Assets (net of debt)	302,610,000	
Brand Value	4,000,000,000	
Total Assets		9,166,130,000

LIABILITIES

Accounts payable	4,400,000	
Loans and mortgages payable on Real and Operating Properties owned 100% by Donald J. Trump		
Commercial Properties (New York City)	321,690,000	
Residential Properties (New York City)	22,190,000	
Club facilities	148,360,000	
Property under development	7,520,000	
Total Liabilities		504,160,000
NET WORTH		8,661,970,000

Exhibit 1c

It was my experience that Mr. Trump inflated his total assets when it served his purposes, such as trying to be listed among the wealthiest people in Forbes, and deflated his assets to reduce his real estate taxes. I am sharing with you two newspaper articles, side by side, that are examples of Mr. Trump inflating and deflating his assets, as I said, to suit his financial interests. These are Exhibit 2 to my testimony. As I noted, I'm giving the Committee today an article he wrote on, and sent me, that reported on an auction of a portrait of Mr. Trump. This is Exhibit 3a to my testimony.

The Guardian

How Trump's $50m golf club became $1.4m when it came time to pay tax

Same Donald Trump-owned golf club is separately accused of causing floods that led to $240,000 worth of damage to New York village of Briarcliff Manor

Jon Swaine *in Briarcliff Manor, New York*
Sat 12 Mar 2016 09.25 EST

An attempt by Donald Trump to slash the property tax bill on a golf club outside New York City may be undermined by records indicating that he previously said the property was worth 35 times more than the value he is now trying to convince a judge to approve.

The Republican presidential frontrunner is suing the town of Ossining in Westchester County to reduce the taxes on Trump National Golf Club, a 147-acre property with a lavish clubhouse and 18-hole course whose managers are separately accused of causing floods that led to $240,000 worth of damage to local public facilities.

Exhibit 2

NY: Donald Trump Announces Presidential Run // Credit: Anthony Behar/Sipa USA/Newscom

Trump Exaggerating His Net Worth (By 100%) In Presidential Bid

Erin Carlyle Forbes Staff
Real estate: markets, luxury homes, and cities.

Campaign exaggerations are as much a part of politics as kissing babies. In announcing his bid for the Republican presidential nomination this morning, Donald Trump started with what *Forbes* believes is a whopper. He claimed his net worth was nearly $9 billion. We figure it's closer to $4 billion -- $4.1 billion to be exact.

This discrepancy is noteworthy, since Trump's financial success – he put his fortune at exactly $8,737,540,000 -- is core to his candidacy. "I'm proud of my net worth. I've done an amazing job," said Trump at his circus-like announcement,

Exhibit 2 (cont.)

Mr. Trump directed me to find a straw bidder to purchase a portrait of him that was being auctioned at an Art Hamptons Event. The objective was to ensure that his portrait, which was going to be auctioned last, would go for the highest price of any portrait that afternoon. The portrait was purchased by the fake bidder for $60,000. Mr. Trump directed the Trump Foundation, which is supposed to be a charitable organization, to repay the fake bidder, despite keeping the art for himself. Please see Exhibit 3b to my testimony.

TRUMP: HIGH ART

Call it the billionaire admiration club. At an ArtHamptons auction, where portraits of **Mick Jagger** and **Donald Trump** were on the block, billionaire art collector **Stewart Rahr** plunked down $60,000 for artist **William Quigley's** painting of The Donald (r.). Quigley's Jagger portrait started at $20,000 and dropped to $10,000 before the artist decided to just keep it.

Exhibit 3a

Donald J. Trump ✔
@realDonaldTrump

Following ⌄

Just found out that at a charity auction of celebrity portraits in E. Hampton, my portrait by artist William Quigley topped list at $60K

7:44 AM - 16 Jul 2013

52 Retweets **37** Likes

💬 150   ⟲ 52   ♡ 37   ✉

Exhibit 3b

And it should come as no surprise that one of my more common responsibilities was that Mr. Trump directed me to call business owners, many of whom were small businesses, that were owed money for their services and told them no payment or a reduced payment would be coming. When I advised Mr. Trump of my success, he actually reveled in it.

And yet, I continued to work for him.

Mr. Trump is a conman.

He asked me to pay off an adult film star with whom he had an affair, and to lie to his wife about it, which I did.

FIRST REPUBLIC BANK
HOME EQUITY LINE OF CREDIT

Statement Period: October 01, 2016 - October 31, 2016
Account Number: ▇▇▇▇▇

PAYMENT AND BALANCE SUMMARY

Current Payment Due	$724.41	Credit Limit	$500,000.00
Past Due Amount	$.00	Available Credit	$118,458.25
Total Payment Due	$724.41	Previous Statement Balance	$251,178.38
Payment Due Date*	11/26/16	Current Statement Balance	$382,266.16

*The Total Payment Due must be received by 3 p.m. on the 11th day after the Payment Due Date or a late charge will be assessed. See your note for your late charge amount.

FINANCE CHARGE	$724.41
Year to Date Interest Paid	$4,562.46

UNLESS DESIGNATED IN THE DETACHABLE COUPON PORTION ABOVE, ANY PAYMENT RECEIVED IN EXCESS OF "TOTAL PAYMENT DUE" WILL BE APPLIED AS A REDUCTION OF PRINCIPAL

ACCOUNT ACTIVITY

DATE	TRANSACTION	AMOUNT	OTHER	FINANCE CHG	PRINCIPAL
	PREVIOUS STATEMENT BALANCE			636.63	250,541.75
10/26	LOAN PAYMENT	636.63-		636.63-	
10/26	007391 ADVANCE	131,000.00			131,000.00
10/31	FINANCE CHG	724.41		724.41	
	CURRENT STATEMENT BALANCE			724.41	381,541.75

DAILY PRINCIPAL BALANCE INFORMATION

DATE	BALANCE	DATE	BALANCE
10/01	250,541.75	10/26	381,541.75

RATE HISTORY

Billing Days 31

DATE	ANNUAL PERCENTAGE RATE	DAILY PERIODIC RATE
10/01	3.100	.000084699

Your APR may vary and is subject to a minimum and maximum rate: Your current minimum APR is 2.850%, and your current maximum APR is 14.950%.

Page 1 of 2

111 PINE STREET, SAN FRANCISCO, CALIFORNIA 94111, TEL (415) 392-1400 OR 1-800-392-1400
24 HOUR AUTOMATED BANKING SYSTEM 1-800-392-1407
www.firstrepublic.com · MEMBER FDIC

FRB 401 - 5/10   15

Exhibit 4

Lying to the First Lady is one of my biggest regrets. She is a kind, good person. I respect her greatly—and she did not deserve that. I am giving the Committee today a copy of the $130,000 wire transfer from me to Ms. Clifford's attorney during the closing days of the presidential campaign that was demanded by Ms. Clifford to maintain her silence about her affair with Mr. Trump. This is Exhibit 4 to my testimony. Mr. Trump directed me to use my own personal funds from a home equity line of credit to avoid any money being traced back to him that could negatively impact his campaign. I did that, too—without bothering to consider whether that was improper, much less whether it was the right thing to do or how it would impact me, my family, or the public.

I am going to jail in part because of my decision to help Mr. Trump hide that payment from the American people before they voted a few days later. As Exhibit 5a to my testimony shows, I am providing a copy of a $35,000 check that President Trump *personally* signed from his *personal* bank account on August 1, 2017—when he was President of the United States—pursuant to the cover-up, which was the basis of my guilty plea, to reimburse me—the word used by Mr. Trump's TV lawyer—for the illegal hush money I paid on his behalf. This $35,000 check was one of 11 check installments that was paid throughout the year—while he was President. Other checks to reimburse me for the hush money payments were signed by Don Jr. and Allen Weisselberg. See, for example, Exhibit 5b.

The President of the United States thus wrote a personal check for the payment of hush money as part of a criminal scheme to violate campaign finance laws. You can find the details of that scheme, directed by Mr. Trump, in the pleadings in the U.S. District Court for the Southern District of New York. So picture this scene—in February 2017, one month into his presidency, I'm visiting President Trump in the Oval Office for the first time. It's truly awe-inspiring, he's showing me around and pointing to different paintings, and he says to me something to the effect of, "Don't worry, Michael, your January and February reimbursement checks are coming. They were Fed-Exed from New York and it takes a while for that to get through the White House system." As he promised, I received the first check for the reimbursement of $70,000 not long thereafter.

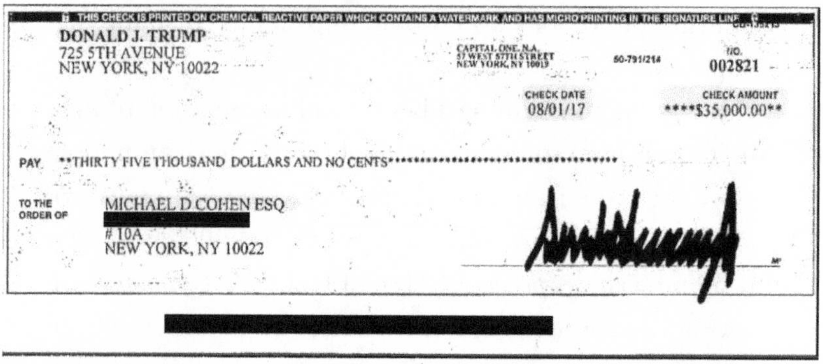

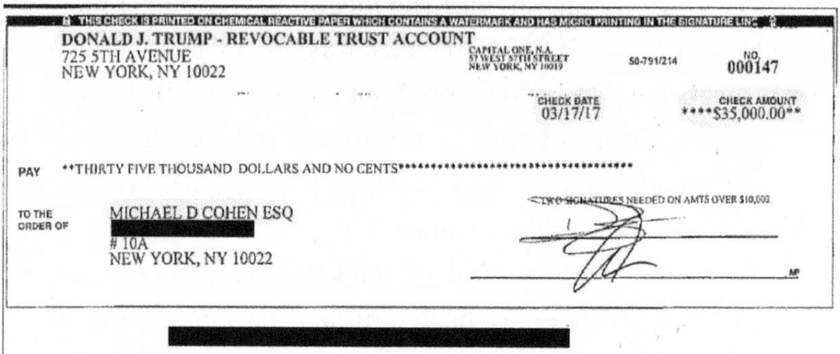

Exhibit 5a

Exhibit 5b

When I say conman, I'm talking about a man who declares himself brilliant but directed me to threaten his high school, his colleges, and the College Board to never release his grades or SAT scores. As I mentioned, I'm giving the Committee today copies of a letter I sent at Mr. Trump's direction threatening these schools with civil and criminal actions if Mr. Trump's grades or SAT scores were ever disclosed without his permission. These are Exhibit 6.

T R U M P

Michael D. Cohen
Executive Vice President and
Special Counsel to
Donald J. Trump
Direct Dial (212) 836-3212
mcohen@trumporg.com

May 5, 2015

BY FEDERAL EXPRESS

Rev. Joseph M. McShane, S.J.
University President
Fordham University- Rose Hill Campus
441 East Fordham Road
Bronx, N.Y 10458

Re: *Records of Donald J. Trump*

Dear Reverend McShane,

Please be advised that I am Executive Vice President and Special Counsel to Donald J. Trump.

It has come to my attention that several media outlets have asked for the release of my client's records. We have turned down these requests.

As I am sure you are aware, pursuant to applicable law, including the Family Educational Rights and Privacy Act (20 U.S.C. § 1232g; 34 CFR Part 99), the release or disclosure, in any form, of such records (or any information contained in such records) to any third party without my client's prior written authorization is expressly prohibited by law, with any violation thereof exposing the subject educational institution to both criminal and civil liability and damages including, among other things, substantial fines, penalties and even the potential loss of government aid and other funding. The criminality will lead to jail time.

Accordingly, please be advised that (i) my client does not consent to any release or disclosure of any educational records to any third parties; and (ii) if in the event any of his records are released or otherwise disclosed without his prior written consent, we will hold your institution liable to the fullest extent of the law including damages and criminality. As you are again no doubt aware, this notice applies to any and all of The College Board's employees, agents, third parties, vendors and any other person or entity acting for or on its behalf.

I thank you for your cooperation. Please guide yourself accordingly and contact me to inform me that the records have been permanently sealed.

Very truly yours,

Michael D. Cohen

P.S. Mr. Trump truly enjoyed his two years at Fordham and has great respect for the University.

Exhibit 6

The irony wasn't lost on me at the time that Mr. Trump in 2011 had strongly criticized President Obama for not releasing his grades. As you can see in Exhibit 7, Mr. Trump declared, "Let him show his records" after calling President Obama "a terrible student."

Trump: Obama a "Terrible Student" Not Good Enough for Harvard

Mogul questions how Obama was accepted to Harvard and Columbia

By Beth Fouhy

Published Apr 25, 2011 at 5:32 PM | Updated at 6:39 AM EDT on Apr 26, 2011

Manhattan real estate mogul Donald Trump suggested in an interview Monday that President Barack Obama had been a poor student who did not deserve to be admitted to the Ivy League universities he attended.

Trump, who is mulling a bid for the Republican presidential nomination, offered no proof for his claim but said he would continue to press the matter as he has the legitimacy of the president's birth certificate.

"I heard he was a terrible student, terrible. How does a bad student go to Columbia and then to Harvard?" Trump said in an interview with The Associated Press. "I'm thinking about it, I'm certainly looking into it. Let him show his records."

Exhibit 7

Obama graduated from Columbia University in New York in 1983 with a degree in political science after transferring from Occidental College in California. He went on to Harvard Law School, where he graduated magna cum laude 1991 and was the first black president of the Harvard Law Review.

Obama's 2008 campaign did not release his college transcripts, and in his best-selling memoir, "Dreams From My Father," Obama indicated he hadn't always been an academic star. Trump told the AP that Obama's refusal to release his college grades were part of a pattern of concealing information about himself.

"I have friends who have smart sons with great marks, great boards, great everything and they can't get into Harvard," Trump said. "We don't know a thing about this guy. There are a lot of questions that are unanswered about our president."

Katie Hogan, a spokeswoman for Obama's re-election campaign, declined to comment.
Trump, a wealthy businessman and reality TV host on NBC, has risen to the top of many polls in part by his outspoken call for Obama to release his long form birth certificate.

The state of Hawaii has released a certificate of live birth indicating Obama was born there on August 4, 1961, but that has not quelled critics who believe Obama was born outside the United States and is therefore not qualified to be president.

The so-called "birther" controversy has dominated the early stage of the 2012 GOP nominating contest, with Trump leading the charge.

"I have more people that are excited about the fact that I reinvigorated this whole issue," Trump said, adding "the last guy (Obama) wants to run against is Donald Trump."

Exhibit 7 (cont.)

Trump is scheduled to travel to the early primary states of New Hampshire and Nevada this week and said he will make a final decision about a presidential bid by June.

Also in the AP interview, Trump:

— Said Republicans had made a mistake by embracing a budget proposal crafted by Wisconsin GOP Rep. Paul Ryan that included deep cuts in Medicare. "The seniors are afraid. The plan Paul Ryan put forth has made the Democrats so happy," Trump said.

— Declined to disclose his net worth, saying he'll do so if he decides to run. "You'll see what it is, possibly, very likely, in the next 4 weeks. I don't want to say because I don't want to ruin the press conference," he said.

— Expressed surprise that the 2008 GOP nominee, John McCain, had suggested Trump's effort was a publicity stunt. "I congratulate him for getting the attention he's getting," McCain told NBC's "Meet the Press" Sunday.

Trump said he had been a big supporter of McCain. "I would find it hard to believe he would say anything bad because I raised a fantastic amount of money for him," Trump said.

https://www.nbcnewyork.com/news/local/Trump-Obama-Wasnt-Good-Enough-to-Get-into-Ivy-Schools-120657869.html

Exhibit 7 (cont.)

The sad fact is that I never heard Mr. Trump say any-thing in private that led me to believe he loved our nation or wanted to make it better. In fact, he did the opposite. When telling me in 2008 that he was cutting employees' salaries in half—including mine—he showed me what he claimed was a $10 million IRS tax refund, and he said that he could not believe how stupid the government was for giving "someone like him" that much money back.

During the campaign, Mr. Trump said he did not con-sider Vietnam veteran and prisoner of war, Senator John McCain to be "a hero" because he likes people who weren't captured. At the same time, Mr. Trump tasked me to han-dle the negative press surrounding his medical deferment from the Vietnam draft. Mr. Trump claimed it was because of a bone spur, but when I asked for medical records, he gave me none and said there was no surgery. He told me not to answer the specific questions by reporters but rather offer simply the fact that he received a medical deferment. He finished the conversation with the following comment. "You think I'm stupid, I wasn't going to Vietnam." I find it ironic, President Trump, that you are in Vietnam right now.

And yet, I continued to work for him.

Questions have been raised about whether I know of di-rect evidence that Mr. Trump or his campaign colluded with Russia. I do not. I want to be clear. But, I have my suspicions.

Sometime in the summer of 2017, I read all over the me-dia that there had been a meeting in Trump Tower in June 2016 involving Don Jr. and others from the campaign with Russians, including a representative of the Russian govern-ment, and an email setting up the meeting with the subject line, "Dirt on Hillary Clinton." Something clicked in my mind. I remember being in the room with Mr. Trump, probably in early June 2016, when something peculiar happened: Don Jr. came into the room and walked behind his father's desk—which in itself was unusual. People didn't just walk behind Mr. Trump's desk to talk to him. I recalled Don Jr. leaning over to his father and speaking in a low voice, which I could clearly hear, and saying: "The meeting is all set." I remember Mr. Trump saying, "Ok good . . . let me know."

What struck me as I looked back and thought about that exchange between Don Jr. and his father was, first, that Mr. Trump had frequently told me and others that his son Don Jr. had the worst judgment of anyone in the world. And also, that Don Jr. would never set up any meeting of any significance alone—and certainly not without checking with his father.

I also knew that nothing went on in Trump world, especially the campaign, without Mr. Trump's knowledge and approval. So, I concluded that Don Jr. was referring to *that* June 2016 Trump Tower meeting about dirt on Hillary with the Russian representative when he walked behind his dad's desk that day—*and* that Mr. Trump knew that was the meeting Don Jr. was talking about when he said, "That's good . . . let me know."

Over the past year or so, I have done some real soul searching. I see now that my ambition and the intoxication of Trump power had much to do with the bad decisions I made. To you, Chairman Cummings, Ranking Member Jordan, the other members of this Committee, and the other members of the House and Senate, I am sorry for my lies and for lying to Congress.

To our nation, I am sorry for actively working to hide from you the truth about Mr. Trump when you needed it most.

For those who question my motives for being here today, I understand. I have lied, but I am not a liar. I have done bad things, but I am not a bad man. I have fixed things, but I am no longer your "fixer," Mr. Trump. I am going to prison and have shattered the safety and security that I tried so hard to provide for my family. My testimony certainly does not diminish the pain I caused my family and friends—nothing can do that. And I have never asked for, nor would I accept, a pardon from President Trump.

And, by coming today, I have caused my family to be the target of personal, scurrilous attacks by the President and his lawyer, trying to intimidate me from appearing before this panel. Mr. Trump called me a "rat" for choosing to tell the truth—much like a mobster would do when one of his men decides to cooperate with the government.

As Exhibit 8 shows, I have provided the Committee with copies of Tweets that Mr. Trump posted, attacking me and my family—only someone burying his head in the sand would not recognize them for what they are: encouragement to someone to do harm to me and my family.

I never imagined that he would engage in vicious, false attacks on my family—and unleash his TV-lawyer to do the same. I hope this committee and all members of Congress on both sides of the aisle will make it clear: As a nation, we should not tolerate attempts to intimidate witnesses before congress and attacks on family are out of bounds and not acceptable.

I wish to especially thank Speaker Pelosi for her statements in Exhibit 9 to protect this institution and me, and the Chairman of the House Permanent Select Committee on Intelligence Adam Schiff and Chairman Cummings for likewise defending this institution and my family against

Donald J. Trump ✓
@realDonaldTrump

Following ⌄

....his wife and father-in-law (who has the money?) off Scott Free. He lied for this outcome and should, in my opinion, serve a full and complete sentence.

7:29 AM - 3 Dec 2018

14,377 Retweets 67,036 Likes

💬 23K   ⟲ 14K   ♡ 67K   ✉

Donald J. Trump ✓
@realDonaldTrump

Following ⌄

Remember, Michael Cohen only became a "Rat" after the FBI did something which was absolutely unthinkable & unheard of until the Witch Hunt was illegally started. They BROKE INTO AN ATTORNEY'S OFFICE! Why didn't they break into the DNC to get the Server, or Crooked's office?

6:39 AM - 16 Dec 2018

31,821 Retweets 126,182 Likes

💬 60K   ⟲ 32K   ♡ 126K   ✉

Exhibit 8

the attacks by Mr. Trump, and also the many Republicans who have admonished the President as well.

I am not a perfect man. I have done things I am not proud of, and I will live with the consequences of my actions for the rest of my life. But today, I get to decide the

Nancy Pelosi ✓
@SpeakerPelosi

(Follow) ∨

Michael Cohen will come before the @OversightDems & @HouseIntel Committees next week. Congress has an independent duty under the Constitution to conduct oversight of the Executive Branch, and any efforts to intimidate family members or pressure witnesses will not be tolerated.

Oversight Committee ✓ @OversightDems
BREAKING NEWS: Chairman @RepCummings announces the rescheduling of Michael Cohen's public testimony for next week, despite efforts by some to intimidate his family members and prevent him from appearing before the Committee.

4:25 PM - 20 Feb 2019

6,634 Retweets **22,234** Likes

♡ 2.4K   ⇄ 6.6K   ♡ 22K   ✉

Exhibit 9

example I set for my children and how I attempt to change how history will remember me. I may not be able to change the past, but I can do right by the American people here today.

Thank you for your attention. I am happy to answer the Committee's questions.

Cummings: Thank you very much, Mr. Cohen. I recognize myself. Mr. Cohen, before I start, I want to make sure you really understand something. You have admitted lying to Congress, to this very body, and now you're going to prison for it. Do you, Mr. Cohen, recognize the gravity of your offenses? You are a lawyer, right?

Cohen: As of yesterday I am no longer a lawyer. I have lost my law license, amongst other things.

Cummings: But you understand the gravity of this moment?

Cohen: I most certainly do, Mr. Chairman.

Cummings: I want you to really hear this, Mr. Cohen. We will not tolerate lying to this Congress by anybody. We are in search of the truth. Do you understand that?

Cohen: I do.

Cummings: Now the President has also made numerous statements that turned out to be inaccurate. For example, he said he knew nothing about the hush money payments to Ms. Clifford. In his 2017 financial disclosure form, said he never owed money to reimburse you for those payments. Yet, in your testimony, Mr. Cohen, you said that you met with the President in the Oval Office in February of 2017 and discussed his plans to reimburse you for money you paid. You say he told you, and I quote, "Don't worry, Michael, your January and February reimbursement checks are coming. Is that accurate? And was that in the Oval Office?

Cohen: The statement is accurate but the discussions regarding the reimbursement occurred long before he became President.

Cummings: Would you explain that?

Cohen: Back in 2017, when—actually I apologize—in 2016, prior to the election, I was contacted by Keith Davidson who is the attorney or was the attorney for Ms. Clifford for Stormy Daniels, and after several rounds of conversations with him about purchasing her life rights for $130,000, what I did each and every time is go straight into Mr. Trump's office and discuss the issue with him. When it was ultimately determined, this was days before the election, that Mr. Trump was going to pay the $130,000, in the office with me was Allen Weisselberg, the chief financial officer of the Trump Organization. He acknowledged to Allen that he was going to pay the $130,000, and that Allen and I should go back to his office and figure out how to do it. So yes, sir, I stand by the statement that I gave, but there was a history to it.

Cummings: In your testimony, you have . . . you said you brought some checks, is that right? You said you brought some checks?

Cohen: Yes, sir.

Cummings: Let me ask you about one of these. This from the Trump trust that holds the President's businesses, can you tell me who signed this check?

Cohen: I believe that the top signature is Donald Trump Jr. And the bottom signature I believe is Allen Weisselberg's.

Cummings: Can you tell me the date of that check?

Cohen: March 17th of 2017.

Cummings: Now wait a minute. Hold up. The date on the check is after President Trump held his big press conference claiming that he gave up control of his businesses? How could the President have arranged for you to get this check if he was supposedly playing no role in his business?

Cohen: Because the payments were designed to be paid over the course of 12 months and it was declared to be a retainer for services that would be provided for the year of 2017.

Cummings: Was there a retainer agreement?

Cohen: There is no retainer agreement.

Cummings: Could Don Jr. or Mr. Weisselberg have more information about that?

Cohen: Mr. Weisselberg for sure about the entire discussions and negotiations prior to the election, and Don Jr. would have cursory information.

Cummings: Now here's another one. This one appears to be signed by Donald Trump himself. Is that his signature?

Cohen: That is Donald Trump's signature.

Cummings: So let me make sure I understand. Donald Trump wrote you a check out of his personal account while he was serving as President of the United States of America to reimburse you for hush money payments to Ms. Clifford? Is that what you are telling the American people today?

Cohen: Yes, Mr. Chairman.

Cummings: One final question: The President claimed he knew nothing about these payments. His ethics filing said he owed nothing to you. Based on your conversations with him, is there any doubt in your mind that President Trump knew exactly what he was paying for?

Cohen: There is no doubt in my mind and I truly believe there is no doubt in the mind of the people of the United States of America.

Cummings: And these new documents appear to corroborate what you just told us. With that I yield to the gentleman from Ohio.

Rep. Jim Jordan (R, Ohio): "I will make sure that you and I meet one day while we're in the courthouse and I will take you for every penny you still don't have and I will come after your Daily Beast and everybody else that you possibly know. I'm warning you, tread very f-ing lightly because what I am going to do to you is going to be f-ing disgusting, do you understand me?" Mr. Cohen, who said that?

Cohen: I did.

Jordan: Did you say that, Mr. Cohen in your testimony on page 2, you said you did things for Mr. Trump in an effort to protect him. Was that statement that I just read that you admitted to saying, did you do that to protect Donald Trump?

Cohen: I did it to protect Mr. Trump, Donald Trump, Jr., Ivanka Trump, and Eric Trump.

Jordan: In your sentencing statement back in December in front of the judge, you said this, Mr. Cohen: "My weakness can be characterized as a blind loyalty to Donald Trump a blind loyalty that led me to choose a path of darkness." Is that right?

Cohen: I wrote that.

Jordan: You wrote and said that in front of the judge.

Cohen: That's correct.

Jordan: Let me read a few other things and ask you why you did some of these things. When you filed a false tax return in 2012, 2013, 2014, 2015, and 2016, was all that out of blind loyalty to the President?

Cohen: No, it was not.

Jordan: When you failed to report $4 million in income to the Internal Revenue Service, did you do that to protect Donald Trump?

Cohen: No, I did not.

Jordan: And when you failed to pay $1.4 million in taxes—I got constituents that don't make that in a lifetime—when you failed to pay $1.4 million in taxes to the U.S. Treasury, was that out of some blind loyalty to the President of the United States?

Cohen: It was not. But the number was $1.38 million and change and I have paid that money back to the IRS at this time.

Jordan: I think the American people appreciate that—

Cohen: I would like to say it was over a course of five years. Approximately $260,000 a year.

Jordan: That's what I said, 2012, 2013, 2014, 2015. That's five years.

Cohen: Yes.

Jordan: Got it. When you made false statements to financial institutions concerning a home equity line of credit, tax medallions on your park avenue apartment in 2013, 2014, 2015, and you pled guilty to making those false statements to those banks, was that all done to protect the President?

Cohen: No, it was not.

Jordan: How about this one: When you created the fake Twitter account, @WomenForCohen, and paid a firm to post tweets like this one: "In a world of lie, deception, and fraud, we appreciate this honest guy @MichaelCohen212. #TGIF #handsome #sexy," was that done to protect the President?

Cohen: Mr. Jordan, I didn't set that up. It was done by a young lady that worked for Redfinch and during the course of the campaign you would know it's somewhat crazy and wild and we were having fun. That's what it was, sir: We were having fun.

Jordan: Was it done to protect the President?

Cohen: That was not done to protect the President.

Jordan: Was it a fake Twitter account?

Cohen: No, that was a real Twitter account. It exists.

Jordan: Did you pay the firm to create this?

Cohen: I didn't pay the firm. It was done by a young lady that works for the firm and again, sir, we were having fun during a stressful time.

Jordan: The point is, Mr. Cohen, did you lie to protect the President or help yourself?

Cohen: I'm not sure how that helped me, sir. More than half the people on that site are men.

Jordan: Here's the point. The Chairman gave you a 30-minute opening statement, and you have a history of lying over and over and over again, and frankly you don't have to take my word for it, take what the court said, take what the Southern District of New York said: Cohen did crimes that were marked by a pattern of deception and that permeated his professional life. These crimes were distinct in their harms but bear a common set of circumstances: They each involve deception and were each, each motivated by personal greed and ambition. A pattern of deception for personal greed and ambition and you just got 30 minutes of an opening statement where you trashed the President of the United States of America. Mr. Cohen, how long did you work for Donald Trump?

Cohen: Approximately a decade.

Jordan: Ten years?

Cohen: That's correct.

Jordan: You said all these bad things about the President there in the last 30 minutes, and yet you worked for him for ten years? I mean, if it's that bad I can see you working for him for ten days, maybe ten weeks, maybe even ten months, but you worked for him for ten years. Mr. Cohen, how long did you work in the White House?

Cohen: I never worked in the White House.

Jordan: That's the point, isn't it, Mr. Cohen?

Cohen: No, sir.

Jordan: Yes, it is.

Cohen: No, it's not, sir.

Jordan: You wanted to work in the White House . . . .

Cohen: No, sir.

Jordan: You didn't get brought to the dance.

Cohen: Sir, I was extremely proud to be personal attorney to the President of the United States of America. I did not want to go to the White House. I was offered jobs. I can tell you a story of Mr. Trump reaming out Reince Priebus because I had not taken a job where Mr. Trump wanted me to, which is working with Don McGahn at the White House general counsel's office. One second. What I said at the time—and I brought a lawyer in who produced a memo as to why I should not go in, because there would be no attorney/client privilege. And in order to handle some of the matters that I talked about in my opening, that it would be best suited for me not to go in and that every President had a personal attorney.

Jordan: Here's what I see. I see a guy who worked for 10 years and is here trashing the guy he worked for for ten years, didn't get a job in the White House, and now, now you're behaving just like everyone else who got fired or didn't get the job they wanted like Andy McCabe, like James Comey, same kind of selfish motivation after you don't get the thing you want. That's what I see here today and I think that's what the American people see.

Cohen: Mr. Jordan, all I wanted was what I got. To be personal attorney to the President, to enjoy the senior year of my son in high school and waiting for my daughter, who is graduating from college, to come back to New York. I got exactly what I want.

Cummings: The gentleman's time has expired. Ms. Wasserman-Schultz.

Rep. Debbie Wasserman-Schultz (D, Florida): Thank you, Mr. Chairman. Mr. Cohen, thank you for being here today. As you likely know I served as the chair of the Democratic National Committee at the time of the Russian hacks and when Russia weaponized the messages that it had stolen, but I want to be clear: My questions are not about the harm done to any individual by WikiLeaks and the Russians. It's about the possible and likely harm to the United States of America and our democracy. I have a series of questions that I hope will connect more of these dots. Mr. Cohen is it your testimony that Mr. Trump had advanced knowledge of the Russia WikiLeaks release of the DNC e-mails?

Cohen: I cannot answer that in a yes or no. He had advanced notice that there was going to be a dump of e-mails, but at no time did I hear the specificity of what those e-mails were going to be.

Wasserman-Schultz: But you do testify today that he had advanced knowledge of their imminent release?

Cohen: That is what I had stated in my testimony.

Wasserman-Schultz: And that he cheered that outcome.

Cohen: Yes, ma'am.

Wasserman-Schultz: Did Mr. Trump likely share this information with his daughter Ivanka, son Don Jr., or Jared Kushner?

Cohen: I'm not aware of that.

Wasserman-Schultz: Was Ivanka, Jared, or Don Jr. still involved in the Russian tower deal at that time?

Cohen: The company was involved in the deal, which meant that the family was involved in the deal.

Wasserman-Schultz: If Mr. Trump and his daughter Ivanka and son Donald Jr. are involved in the Russian Trump Tower deal, is it possible the whole family is conflicted or compromised with a foreign adversary in the months before the election?

Cohen: Yes.

Wasserman-Schultz: Based on your experience with the President and knowledge of his relationship with Mr. Stone, do you have reason to believe that the President explicitly or implicitly authorized Mr. Stone to make contact with WikiLeaks and to indicate the campaign's interest in the strategic release of these illegally hacked materials.

Cohen: I'm not aware of that.

Wasserman-Schultz: Was Mr. Stone a free agent reporting back to the President what he had done? Or was he an agent of the campaign acting on behalf of the President and with his apparent authority?

Cohen: No. He was a free agent.

Wasserman-Schultz: A free agent that was reporting back to the President what he had done?

Cohen: Correct. He frequently reached out to Mr. Trump and Mr. Trump was very happy to take his calls. It was free service.

Wasserman-Schultz: Roger stone says he never spoke with Mr. Trump about WikiLeaks. How can we corroborate what you are saying?

Cohen: I don't know, but I suspect that the Special Counsel's office and other government agencies have the information that you're seeking.

Wasserman-Schultz: Moving to later in 2016, a major WikiLeaks dump happened hours after the "Access Hollywood" tape was released.

Cohen: I am unaware of that. I actually was not even in the country at the time of the Billy Bush tape. I was in London visiting my daughter. . . .

Wasserman-Schultz: Knowing how Mr. Trump operates with his winning-at-all-costs mentality, do you believe that he would cooperate or collude with a foreign power to win the presidency? Is he capable of that?

Cohen: It calls on so much speculation, ma'am. It would be unfair for me to . . . .

Wasserman-Schultz: I understand. You have a tremendous amount of experience.

Cohen: Mr. Trump is all about winning. He will do what is necessary to win.

Wasserman-Schultz: In your opinion and experience, would he have the potential to collude with a foreign power to win the presidency at all costs?

Cohen: Yes.

Wasserman-Schultz: Based on what you know, would Mr. Trump or did he lie about colluding and coordinating with the Russians at any point during the campaign?

Cohen: So as I stated in my testimony, I wouldn't use the word *colluding*. Was there something odd about the back and forth praise with President Putin, yes. But I'm not really sure that I can answer that question in terms of collusion. I was not part of the campaign. I don't know the other conversations that Mr. Trump had with other individuals. There's just so many dots that all seem to lead to the same direction.

Wasserman-Schultz: Finally, before my time expires, Mr. Cohen, the campaign and the entire Trump Organization appeared to be filthy with Russian contact. There are Russian business contacts, there are campaign Russian contacts, there are lies about all of those contacts, and then we have Roger Stone informing the President just before the Democratic National Convention that these—that WikiLeaks was going to drop documents in the public arena that we knew at that point were hacked and stolen by Russia from the Democratic National Committee.

Cummings: The gentlelady's time has expired. You may answer her inquiry.

Wasserman-Schultz: My question is . . . .

Cummings: Quickly.

Wasserman-Schultz: Given all those connections, is it likely that Donald Trump was fully aware and had every intent of working with Russia to help make sure he could win the presidency at all costs?

Cohen: So let me say that this is a matter that's currently being handled by the House Select and Senate Select Intelligence committees, as I would rather not answer that specific question other than just to tell you that Mr. Trump's desire to win would have him work with anyone. And one other thing that I had said in my statement is that when it came to the Trump Tower Moscow project, it was worth hundreds of millions of dollars, and we never expected to win the election, so this was just business as usual.

Cummings: Representative Mark Green of Tennessee.

Wasserman-Schultz: All right. Thank you, Mr. Chairman.

Rep. Mark Green (R, Tennessee): Thank you, Mr. Chairman. Ranking Member Jordan, chairman in this committee, promised the American people a fair and open process, yet the Democrats have limited the scope of this hearing. They've issued a gag order to tell members of this committee what we can and cannot talk about. My colleagues on the other side of the aisle claim that they want the truth, that they want transparency and fair oversight, yet the Democrats' witness to testify before Congress today is none other than a scorned man who is going to prison for lying to Congress. Let that sink in. He's going to prison for lying to Congress. And he's the star witness to Congress. If you read the sentencing report on Michael Cohen, words like *deceptive* and *greedy* are scattered throughout that report. It paints a picture of a narcissist, a bully who cannot tell the truth whether it's about the President or about his own personal life. But today, he's the majority party's star witness. If the Democrats were after the truth, they would have an honest person here testifying. And if they were really after the truth, they would not restrict the questioning to just a few topics, but let's take a look at those restricted topics.

Mr. Chairman, the first topic in your limited scope I can ask Mr. Cohen is about the President's debts. But Mr. Chairman, didn't Mr. Cohen plead guilty to lying to banks about his personal finances? So we're asking a guy going to jail for lying about his debts to comment about the President's debts. He's the expert. Mr. Chairman, your next couple of topics say that I can ask Mr. Cohen about the President's compliance with financial disclosures and campaign finance laws, but didn't Mr. Cohen on two occasions break campaign finance law with his own donation? Again, the majority party's star witness on the President's compliance is a guy who broke compliance laws himself.

Mr. Chairman, you graciously allow us to ask questions of Mr. Cohen on the President's dealings with the IRS and tax law. Your star witness here broke the law with regards to the IRS at least five times. He pled guilty on cheating on his taxes, lying to the IRS, and he's the best witness you got. Next up, with the permission of the chairman, I get to ask Mr. Cohen about his perspective on the President's business dealings. Let me get this straight: the witness lied to multiple financial institutions to get loans to pay off other loans just to keep himself afloat, and he's going to be the expert on business practices. Obviously, Mr. Chairman, the witness may produce documents he suggests incriminates the President, yet he lies to banks. All of those lies were done on fraudulent documents, documents that he forged. Nothing he says or produces has any credibility. Apparently he even lied about delivering his own child, which his wife had to correct for the record.

Ladies and gentlemen, how on earth is this witness credible? With all the lies and deception, the self-serving fraud, it begs the question: What is the majority party doing here? No one can see this guy as credible. He will say whatever he wants to accomplish his own personal goals. He's a fake witness. And his presence here is a travesty. I hope the American people see through this. I know the people back in Tennessee will. And with that statement, sir, I have a few questions of the witness. With your loss of your law license—I think you mentioned in your opening statement you had been disbarred—what is your source of income in the future?

Cohen: I don't expect I'm going to have a source of income when I'm in federal penitentiary.

Green: What . . . Is there a book deal coming or anything like that?

Cohen: I have no book deal right now in the process. I have been contacted by many, including for television and movie. If you want to tell me who you would like to play you, I'm more than happy to write the name down.

Green: I'm sure there's a very . . . .

Cohen: I would like to correct your statement on me.

Green: No . . . Let me ask one other question I only have a limited amount of time. Who paid your expenses to be here today?

Cohen: Who's paid my expenses?

Green: To be here today.

Cohen: I paid my expenses.

Green: Mr. Chairman, I would like to yield the remaining of my time to the ranking member.

Jordan: Mr. Cohen, how many times did you talk to the Special Counsel's office?

Cohen: Seven.

Jordan: Did they talk to you at all in preparation for today's hearing between the seven times you talked to them prior to your sentencing, have you had any conversations with the Special Counsel's office between sentencing and today?

Cohen: I'm sorry, sir, I don't understand your question.

Jordan: You talked to them seven times in the sentencing memorandums in front of the court back in December. What I'm asking is how many times have you talked to the Special Counsel's office since then up to today's appearance here in Congress?

Cummings: The gentleman's time has expired. You may answer that one question, though.

Cohen: I'm sorry, I don't have the answer to that.

Rep. Carolyn Maloney (D, New York): Thank you, Mr. Chairman. Mr. Cohen, in your ten years of working for Donald Trump, did he control everything that went on in the Trump Organization, and did you have to get his permission in advance and report back after every meeting of any importance?

Cohen: Yes. There was nothing that happened at the Trump Organization, from whether it was a response as the

Daily Beast story you referred to, Ranking Member, that did not go through Mr. Trump with his approval. And sign off. As in the case of the payments.

Maloney: How many times did the President, Michael, ask you or direct you to try to reach settlements with women in 2015 and 2016?

Cohen: I'm sorry, ma'am, I don't have the answer to that. I would have to go back and try to recollect. It's certainly the two that we know about.

Maloney: And why do you think the President did not provide the accurate information in his 2017 financial disclosure form? What was he trying to hide? He corrected other forms but he didn't correct this one.

Cohen: The payments on the reimbursement of the funds that I extended on his behalf.

Maloney: Can you elaborate more?

Cohen: Well, going back into the story as I stated when we—Allen Weisselberg and I—left the office and went to his office to make the determination on how the money was going to be wired to the IOLA, the interest on the lawyer's account for Keith Davidson in California. I had asked Allen to use his money. I didn't want to use mine. He said he couldn't. We then decided how else we could do it, and he asked me whether or not I know anybody that wants to have a party at one of his clubs that could pay me instead, or somebody who may have wanted to become a member of one of the golf clubs. And I also don't have anybody that was interested in that. And it got to the point where it was down to the wire. It was either somebody wire the funds and purchase the life rights to the story from Ms. Clifford, or it was going to end up being sold to television, and that would have embarrassed the President, and it would have interfered with the election.

Maloney: But the President has never amended his 2017 form to this day, and while you're facing the consequences of going to jail, he is not.

Cohen: I believe that they amended a financial disclosure form and there's a footnote somewhere, buried. I don't recall specifically what it says. But there is a footnote buried somewhere.

Maloney: Can you describe, Michael, to the American people "catch and kill"?

Cohen: So "catch and kill" is a method that exists when you are working with a news outlet—in this specific case it was AMI, *National Enquirer,* David Pecker, Dylan Howard, and others—where they would contact me or Mr. Trump or someone and state that there's a story that's percolating out there that you may be interested in. And then what you do is you contact that individual and you purchase the rights to that story from them.

Maloney: And you practiced this for the President?

Cohen: I was involved in several of these catch-and-kill episodes, but these catch-and-kill scenarios existed between David Pecker and Mr. Trump long before I started working for him in 2007.

Maloney: Michael, can you suggest who else this committee should talk to for additional information on this or anything else?

Cohen: Yes. I believe David Pecker, Dylan Howard, Barry Levine of AMI as well. Alan Weisselberg, Alan Garten at the Trump Organization as well.

Maloney: Thank you very much for your testimony. And Mr. Chairman, this is a story of redemption.

Cummings: Thank you, ma'am. Mr. Comer.

Rep. James Comer (R, Kentucky): Mr. Cohen, in your testimony, you stated that you began work for the Trump Organization as a lawyer dealing with real estate transactions. Is that correct?

Cohen: That's correct.

Comer: Prior to coming to Congress I served as a director of two different banks, so I've seen hundreds of loan applications and, to try to determine your credibility today, I want to ask you a couple of real estate transaction questions to see how, in fact, you operate. According to the Southern District of New York prosecutors, you lied to banks to secure loans by falsely stating the amount of debt you were carrying. Mr. Cohen, my question to you: Was it Donald Trump's fault that you knowingly committed a crime of deception to defraud a bank?

Cohen: No, it's not.

Comer: Was that fraudulent loan you obtained for the Trump Organization or for you personally?

Cohen: It would be for me, though I'm not familiar with which loan that you're referring to. I will—I would like to say one thing, Mr.—sorry, I would like to respond. When you are talking about the home equity line of credit, which is what I believe you're referring to . . . .

Comer: We're also referring to the loan pertaining to your summer home you purchased.

Cohen: I never purchased a summer home. No individual, or no bank, in the 22 years that I've had loans have ever lost a dollar with me. I owe no money to any bank.

Comer: The banks usually find out if someone is trying to deceive them.

Cohen: In 22 years I have no money that's ever been owed to any individual or any bank.

Comer: Did your so-called blind loyalty to the President cause you to defraud the bank for your own personal gain?

Cohen: I take exception to that because there's never been a fraud—I never defrauded any bank.

Comer: Let's dig deeper on that on the bank fraud. According to the Southern District of New York you failed to disclose more than $20 million in liabilities as well as tens of thousands of dollars of monthly expenses. That's according to the Southern District of New York. Now, Mr. Cohen, you being a lawyer, surely you knew you were breaking the law. Why would you have done that?

Cohen: I'm not a CPA and I pled guilty. I'm going to prison as a result of it.

Comer: Because you're a con?

Cohen: No, sir, because I pled guilty, and I am going to be doing the time. I have caused tremendous, tremendous pain to my family and I take no happiness in the . . . .

Comer: One last question about the bank: When the bank found out about the liabilities that you failed to disclose, you lied again to the bank, this is according to the Southern District of New York, and said it had been expunged when, in fact, you shifted the debt to another bank. So apparently, according to the information that we received, your intent to defraud the bank was for the desire to purchase the summer home for $8.5 million?

Cohen: No, sir. That would have been off of an equity line, considering I had less than a 50% loan to value on the assets, and it was a preexisting line of credit that existed years before the date that you're referring to, where this is all surrounding New York City taxi medallions.

Comer: You understand that when you failed to disclose liabilities—especially $20 million in liabilities—that is, in fact, fraud?

Cohen: Except even with the $20 million in liability . . . .

Comer: How much was it?

Cohen: The medallions at that time were worth over $45 million.

Comer: Mr. Cohen, you called Donald Trump a cheat in your opening testimony. What would you call yourself?

Cohen: A fool.

Comer: You calling—okay. Well no comment on that.

Cohen: I appreciate it.

Comer: Mr. Chairman, we said we were in search of the truth. I don't believe that Michael Cohen is capable of telling the truth, and I would hope that as this Committee moves forward that when we have the opportunity to subpoena witnesses . . . that are not recently disbarred, are not convicted felon, and witnesses that haven't committed bank fraud and tax fraud. That is how we're going to determine the truth. Mr. Chairman, I yield the balance of my time to the Ranking Member.

Jordan: I would just make one point. We just had a five-minute debate where Mr. Cohen disputes what is the Southern District of New York found, what the judge found, that he was actually guilty of committing bank fraud. If this statement back here doesn't say it all, Cohen's consciousness of wrongdoing is fleeting, his instinct to blame others is strong. His remorse is nonexistent. He just debated a member of Congress saying I really didn't do anything wrong—

Cohen: Mr. Jordan, that's not what I said. And you know that's not what I said . . . I said that I pled guilty and I take responsibility for my actions . . . . Shame on you, Mr. Jordan. That's not what I said. Shame on you. Mr. Chairman, that's not what I said. What I said is I took responsibility and I take responsibility. What I was doing is explaining to the gentleman that his facts are inaccurate. I still—I take responsibility for my mistakes. All right. I am remorseful. And I am going to prison. I will be away from my wife and family for years, so before you turn around and you cast more dispersion, please understand, there are people watching you today that know me a whole lot better. I made mistakes. I own them. And I didn't fight with the Southern District of New York. I didn't put the system through an entire scenario, but what I did do is I pled guilty and I am going to be, again, going to prison.

Cummings: Ms. Norton.

Rep. Eleanor Holmes Norton (D, District of Columbia): Mr. Cohen, at the center the reasons you're going to prison is conviction for campaign finance violations, and they center around some salacious revelations. The *Washing-*

ton Post reported or aired an "Access Hollywood" video. It set a record for the number of people who watched, crashed the newspaper's server. But this happened in early October on the cusp of the election. What was Mr. Trump's reaction to the video becoming public at that time, and was he concerned about the impact of that video on the election?

Cohen: The answer is yes. As I stated before, I was in London at the time, visiting my daughter who was studying there for a Washington semester abroad, and I received a phone call during the dinner from Hope Hicks, stating that she had just spoken to Mr. Trump and we need you to start making phone calls to the various different news outlets you have relationships with and we need to spin this and what we want to do is just claim this was men locker room talk.

Norton: Was the concern about the election in particular?

Cohen: The answer is yes. Then couple that with Karen McDougal, which then came out around the same time, and then, on top of that, the Stormy Daniels matter.

Norton: Yeah. And these things happened in the month before the election and almost one after the other. The Stormy Daniels revelation, where prosecutors and officials . . . prosecutors learned of that matter, and prosecutors stated that the officials at the magazine contacted you about the story and . . . the magazine, of course, is the *National Enquirer.* Is that correct? They did come to you?

Cohen: Yes, ma'am.

Norton: Were you concerned about this news story becoming public right after the "Access Hollywood" story in terms of impact on the election?

Cohen: I was concerned about it, but more importantly, Mr. Trump was concerned about it.

Norton: That was my next question. What was the President's concern about these matters becoming public in October as we were about to go into an election?

Cohen: I don't think anybody would dispute this belief that after the wildfire that encompassed the Billy Bush tape, that a second follow-up to it would not have been pleasant, and he was concerned with the effect that it had had on the campaign on how women were seeing him and ultimately whether or not he would have a shot in the general election.

Norton: So you negotiated the $130,000 payment.

Cohen: The $130,000 number was not a number that was actually negotiated. It was told to me by Keith Davidson that this is a number that Ms. Clifford wanted.

Norton: You finally completed that deal as it were on October 25th.

Cohen: 28th.

Norton: Days before the election. What happened in the interim?

Cohen: Contemplated whether or not to do it. Wasn't sure if she was really going to go public. It was again some communications back and forth between myself and Keith Davidson. Ultimately it came to either do it or don't and, I had gone into Mr. Trump's office after I had done after each and every conversation, and he told me he had spoken to a couple friends, it's $130,000, not a lot of money, and we should just go ahead and do it. At the time I was with Allen Weisselberg . . . He directed us to go back to Mr. Weisselberg's office and figure this all out.

Norton: Thank you, Mr. Chairman.

Cummings: Mr. Meadows.

Rep. Mark Meadows (R, North Carolina): Mr. Cohen, do you know Lynn Patton? I'm right here.

Cohen: Yes, sir.

Meadows: Mr. Cohen, do you know Lynne Patton?

Cohen: Yes, I do.

Meadows: I asked Lynn to come today in her personal capacity to shed some light. How long have you known Ms. Patton?

Cohen: I'm responsible for Ms. Patton joining the Trump Organization in the job that she currently holds.

Meadows: Well, I'm glad you acknowledge that because you made some very demeaning comments about the President that Ms. Patton doesn't agree with. In fact, it has to do with your claim of racism. She says that as a daughter of a man born in Birmingham, Alabama, that there is no way that she would work for an individual who was racist. How do you reconcile the two of those?

Cohen: And neither should I as the son of a Holocaust survivor.

Meadows: But, Mr. Cohen, I guess what I'm saying is, is I've talked to the President over 300 times. I've not heard one time a racist comment out of his mouth in private, so how do you reconcile it? Do you have proof of those conversations?

Cohen: I would ask you to ask—

Meadows: Do you have tape recordings of those conversations?

Cohen: No, sir.

Meadows: You taped everybody else, so why—

Cohen: That's not true.

Meadows: You haven't taped anybody.

Cohen: I have taped individuals—

Meadows: How many times have you taped individuals?

Cohen: Maybe 100 times over ten years.

Meadows: Is that a low estimate? I've heard it's over 200 times.

Cohen: I don't think . . .I think it's about 100 from what I recall. You asked me a question. Here's—

Meadows: Do you have proof, yes or no?

Cohen: I do.

Meadows: Where's the proof?

Cohen: Ask Ms. Patton how many people who are black are executives at the Trump Organization? And the answer is zero.

Meadows: Mr. Cohen, we can go through this. Here—

Cohen: You asked me.

Meadows: I would ask unanimous consent her entire statement be put in the record.

Cummings: Without objection.

Meadows: Let me go on a little further. Did you collect $1.2 million or so from Novartis?

Cohen: I did.

Meadows: For access to the Trump Administration?

Cohen: No, sir.

Meadows: Why did you collect it?

Cohen: Because they came to me based upon my knowledge of the enigma Donald Trump, what he thinks—

Meadows: They paid you.

Cohen: Let me finish.

Meadows: Did they pay you $1.2 million to give them advice?

Cohen: Yes, they did. Multibillion-dollar conglomerate came to me looking for information, not something that's unusual here in D.C., looking for information and they believed that I had a value.

Meadows: How many times did you meet with them?

Cohen: That value was the insight I was capable of offering them, and they were willing to pay.

Meadows: How many times did you meet with them for $1.2 million? How many times did you meet with them?

Cohen: I provided them with both in person as well as telephone access whenever they needed.

Meadows: How many times? That's a question, Mr. Cohen.

Cohen: I don't recall, sir.

Meadows: Did you ever talk to them?

Cohen: I spoke to them on several occasions.

Meadows: How many?

Cohen: Six times.

Meadows: Six times. Wow. $200,000 a call.

Cohen: Sir, I also would like to—

Meadows: Hold on.

Cohen: I would like to bring your attention—

Meadows: This is my five minutes and not yours. Did you get money from the bank of Kazakhstan?

Cohen: It's not a bank of Kazakhstan. It's called BTA.

Meadows: BTA Bank. Did you get money from them?

Cohen: I did.

Meadows: For what purpose?

Cohen: The purpose was because the former CEO of that bank had absconded with over—it was between $4 to $6 billion, and some of that money was here in the United States, and they sought my assistance in terms of finding, locating that money and helping them to recollect it.

Meadows: So are you saying that all the reports that you were paid in some estimates over $4 million to have access and understanding of the Trump Administration, you're saying all of that was just paid to you just because you're a nice guy?

Cohen: I am a nice guy, but more importantly—

Meadows: I would beg to differ. The record reflects that you're not a nice guy.

Cohen: Each and every contract contained the clause in my contracts said I will not lobby and I could not do government relations work. In fact, in fact, Novartis sent me their contract, which stated specifically that they wanted me to lobby, that they wanted me to provide access to government, including the President. That information, that paragraph was crossed out by me, initialed and written in my own handwriting that says I will not lobby or do government relations work.

Meadows: So Novartis representatives say it was like they were hiring a nonregistered lobbyist. So you disagree with that?

Cohen: I don't know what they said, sir, but the contract speaks for itself.

Meadows: Have you ever contacted anybody in the administration?

Cohen: Yes.

Meadows: To advocate on behalf of any aspect of any of your contracts?

Cummings: The gentleman's time—

Meadows: I ask unanimous consent, I ask unanimous consent—

Cummings: The gentleman's time has expired. You may answer the question.

Cohen: I don't know what you're referring to, sir.

Meadows: Mr. Chairman—

Cummings: Mr. Clay.

Rep. Lacy Clay (D, Missouri): Thank you, Mr. Chairman. Mr. Cohen, I'm pleased you agreed to testify today voluntarily. In my view we are all here for just one reason, and that's the American people are tired of being lied to. They have been lied to by President Trump, they've been lied to by the President's children, they have been lied to by the President's legal representatives. It pains me to say that they have been even lied to by his congressional enablers who are still devoted to perpetuating and protecting this giant con game on the American people. Now Mr. Cohen, I would like to talk to you about the President's assets. Since by law these must be reported accurately on his federal financial disclosure and when he submits them for a bank loan. Mr. Cohen, you served for nearly a decade as then businessman Trump's personal attorney and so-called fixer. Did you also have an understanding of the President's assets and how he valued those items?

Cohen: Yes.

Clay: In November of 2017, *Crain's New York Business* reported that the Trump Organization provided, quote, flagrantly untrue revenue figures going back to at least 2010 to influence Crain's ranking of the largest private companies in New York. According to the reports, while the Trump Organization reported nearly $9.5 billion in revenues in 2016, public filings suggest revenues were less than one tenth of that. To your knowledge, did the President or his company ever inflate assets or revenues?

Cohen: Yes.

Clay: Was that done with the President's knowledge or direction?

Cohen: Everything was done with the knowledge and at the direction of Mr. Trump.

Clay: Tell us why he would do that and what purpose did it serve.

Cohen: It depends upon the situation. There were times that I was asked, again with Allen Weisselberg, the CFO, to go back to speak with an individual from Forbes, because Mr. Trump wanted each year to have his net worth rise on the Forbes wealthiest individuals list. And so what you do is you look at the assets and you try to find an asset that has say, for example, 40 Wall Street, which is about 1.2 million square feet. Find an asset that is comparable, find the highest price per square foot that's achieved in the area and apply it to that building. Or if you're going off of your rent roll, go by the gross rent roll times a multiple and you make up the multiple which is something he had talked about. It's based upon what he wanted to value the asset at.

Clay: You have provided this committee with copies of the President's financial statements or parts of them from 2011, 2012, and '13, and Mr. Chairman I would like to submit those for the record. Mr. Chairman, I would like to submit the statements to the record.

Cummings: Without objection, so ordered.

Clay: Thank you . . . . Can you explain why you had these financial statements and what you used them for? These were used by me for two purposes, one was discussing with media whether *Forbes* or other magazines to demonstrate Mr. Trump's significant net worth. That was one function. Another was when we were dealing later on with insurance companies, we would provide them with copies so that they would understand that the premium on the individual's capabilities to pay would be reduced. And all of this was done at the President's direction and with his knowledge?

Cohen: Yes, because whatever the numbers would come back to be, we would immediately report it back.

Clay: And did this information provided to us inflate the president's assets?

Cohen: I believe these numbers are inflated.

Clay: And, of course—inflating assets to boost your ego is not a crime, but to your knowledge did the president ever provide inflated assets it to a bank in order to obtain a loan?

Cummings: The gentleman's time has expired but you may answer that question.

Cohen: These documents and others were provided to Deutsch Bank on one occasion where I was with them in our attempt to obtain money so that we can put a bid on the Buffalo Bills.

Clay: Thank you for your answer.

Cummings: Mr. Hice of Georgia.

Rep. Jody Hice (R, Georgia): I would like to yield to the gentleman from North Carolina.

Meadows: I thank the gentleman for yielding and ask unanimous consent to put into the record an article from state which indicates that Mr. Cohen's promised access— not just Trump but also the circle around him—it was almost as if we were hiring a lobbyist. I ask unanimous consent.

Cummings: Without objection.

Meadows: I ask unanimous consent that we put into the record a criminal referral for violating section 22 USC of the statute number 611. I ask unanimous consent that my letter referring Mr. Cohen for violating FARA, for illegal lobbying activity, be entered into the record.

Cummings: Without objection.

Meadows: I ask unanimous consent that the first order of business for this committee is for us to look in a bipartisan way at criminal referrals at the next business meeting.

Cummings: These are not documents. They're objections. They're objections.

Meadows: So we're objecting to a unanimous consent request? Is that what, Mr. Chairman?

Cummings: Yes.

Meadows: I will yield back.

Cummings: All right. Let me be clear, Mr. Hice, I'm going to give you your whole five minutes in fairness to you.

Hice: Thank you, Mr. Chairman.

Cummings: And Mr. Meadows, the chairman the ranking member made me aware that I had given a little more time to Ms. Wasserman-Schultz. I was going to let you do that anyway. But I just want the committee to know that because of Wasserman-Schultz I'm going to be strict on the five minutes. Thank you very much. Mr. Hice, you have five minutes.

Hice: Thank you, Mr. Chairman. Mr. Cohen, you've claimed that you've lied, but you're not a liar. To set the record straight, if you've lied, you are a liar by definition. You also said a moment ago that the facts are inaccurate. If they are facts, they are accurate, and that would make you inaccurate. But I would like to know who you consulted with for today's hearing. Lanny Davis and who else?

Cohen: My counsel, Lanny Davis as well as Michael Monaco.

Hice: Did you or any of them cooperate with the Democratic majority in preparing for this meeting?

Cohen: I'm sorry, say that again, please?

Hice: Did you or anyone else on your team cooperate with the Democratic party in preparing for this?

Cohen: We've spoken to the party.

Hice: Did you prepare with Chairman Cummings?

Cohen: I'm sorry, what do you mean by "prepare"? I prepared with my counsel.

Hice: Did you prepare with the Democratic party or Chairman Cummings?

Cohen: We spoke with Chairman Cummings and the party.

Hice: With Chairman Schiff?

Cohen: With Chairman Schiff and his people as well.

Hice: Were there any other individuals acting as a liaison for you with the majority party?

Cohen: I'm sorry, sir, what are you saying?

Hice: Did you have a liaison working with you to prepare for this meeting?

Cohen: We spoke with the various individuals you just raised. yes.

Hice: Tom Steyer. Regarding him or any representatives, is he or any of them paying Lanny Davis to represent you?

Cohen: Not that I'm aware of.

Hice: Who is paying Lanny Davis?

Cohen: At the moment, no one.

Hice: He is doing all this work for nothing?

Cohen: Yes, sir, and I hope so.

Hice: How did Lanny Davis come to you?

Cohen: I reached out to him at the suggestion of my former counsel who knew him.

Hice: So you reached out to Mr. Davis?

Cohen: Yes, I did initially.

Hice: Okay. Did you want to testify before Congress, or did he urge you to testify here?

Cohen: I was asked to come here. I am here, sir, voluntarily.

Hice: Did he ask you to come here?

Cohen: No, sir.

Hice: He says that he did ask you to come here and he convinced you and he did the same with Chairman Cummings as well. So your testimony here is that you approached Lanny Davis to represent you and to come here. He did not persuade you to come here.

Cohen: He did not persuade me. Actually Chairman\Cummings, which is part of the conversations we engaged in, as well as Chairman Schiff and others. They spoke in order to ask me to come here voluntarily.

Hice: I find the connecting. Dots here with Mr. Davis and you and frankly the Chairman and perhaps others to be rather stunning that there is an agenda for all of this happening here today. I believe frankly, that is to bring the President down. You made an oath last time you were here. That oath meant nothing to you then. We had an oath here in this very room about a month ago. It was, quote, be clear that I will speak the truth, nothing but the truth, so help me God. End quote. Sounds like an oath to me. The Chairman made that oath in this room. Here we are today, our first big hearing with you, as we all know a convicted liar, lying to Congress, a criminal. I believe this witness is totally incompatible with the stated goal of seeking the truth in this hearing. This is the first time in the history of Congress we have someone testifying here who has been convicted of lying to Congress. So congratulations for being the first. Mr. Cummings as well. We have brought this committee to its knees in terms of losing its credibility. It is a shameful mockery of what our purpose is. I yield back.

Cummings: Mr. Lynch.

Rep. Stephen Lynch (D, Massachusetts): Let me pick up on those last comments. I want to talk about a low point. Mr. Papadopoulos pled guilty, Mr. Manafort convicted of two other charges, Mr. Gates pled guilty, Mr. Flynn pled guilty, Mr. Pinedo pled guilty . . . Mr. Kilimnik indicted for obstruction of justice. For two years, you want to talk about an agenda, my friends on the other side of the aisle refuse to bring any of these people up before the committee. Today, we have one witness who voluntarily is coming forward to testify. Your side ran away from the truth. We are trying to bring it to the American people. So Mr. Cohen, thank you for voluntarily coming before the committee to testify.

I want to ask you about your statements regarding Trump Tower and Moscow. You may not be aware of it, but this goes back a ways. In 1987, Mr. Trump wrote that he had ongoing discussions with Soviet officials to build a large luxury hotel across from the Kremlin. In partnership with the Soviet Union. At that time, it was the Soviet Union. I want to ask you, in your filing with the Special Counsel Mueller's office, the prosecutors wrote, and I quote, "Mr. Cohen discussed the status and progress of the Moscow Project with Individual 1 on more than the three occasions Mr. Cohen claimed to the committee, and he briefed family members of Individual 1 about the project." Who are we referring to here as Individual 1?

Cohen: Donald J. Trump.

Lynch: And the company?

Cohen: The Trump Organization, through a subsidiary.

Lynch: And who are the family members you briefed on the project?

Cohen: Don Trump Jr. and Ivanka Trump.

Lynch: Were these are the regular course of business or did they request the briefing?

Cohen: This is the regular course of business.

Lynch: Do you recall how many of these briefings there might have been?

Cohen: Approximately ten in total.

Lynch: You also wrote, I quote, "There are at least a half dozen times between the Iowa caucus the end of 2016 and the end of June when Mr. Trump would ask me, how is it going in Russia?" How did the president communicate those questions to you? Was it verbally or over the phone?

Cohen: Verbally mostly all of the time. He would say, "Michael, come walk with me." He was heading to a rally or a car. As I would walk him to the elevator, he would ask me questions quickly regarding the series of issues.

Lynch: Any doubt what he was referring to about the project in Russia?

Cohen: No. This would be it. Otherwise there would have been no reason to ask it of me.

Lynch: You wrote, quote, "Mr. Trump knew of and directed the negotiations throughout the campaign and lied about it," closed quote. How did the President actually direct the negotiations?

Cohen: After each communication I had, I would report back to him. Our goal was to get this project. We were interested in building what would have been the largest building in all of Europe. If I can say one last thing, this is on topic. The lies that I told to congress in fairness benefitted Mr. Trump. In furtherance of my protection of Mr. Trump, which I stated in my testimony. I am not protecting Mr. Trump anymore. While I truly appreciate taking some of your time onto it, to attack me every single time about taxes, that I had no credibility, it is for exactly that reason I spent the last week searching boxes to find the information that I did, so you don't have to take my word for it. I don't want you to. Look at the documents and make your own decision.

Lynch: Let me just say I don't think my colleagues on the other side of the aisle are afraid you are going to lie. I think they are afraid you are going to tell the truth.

Cohen: Thank you, sir.

Lynch: I yield the balance of my time.

Cummings: Thank you very much. Mr. Gosar.

Rep. Paul Gosar (R, Arizona): The gentleman from Ohio is recognized.

Rep. Jim Jordan (R, Ohio): I appreciate the gentleman for yielding. I just want to respond to Mr. Lynch. When have you ever seen a federal agency where this happened: James Comey, director, fired, Andy McCabe, deputy director, fired, lied three times under oath, under investigation as we speak. Jim Baker, FBI counsel demoted then left. Currently under investigation by the U.S. Attorney's office in Connecticut. Lisa Page demoted then left. Peter Struck, director of counterintelligence, demoted then fired. That's what happened. That's what we're concerned about. We asked for Rob Rosenstein . . . . We now know three people have told us Rob Rosenstein was actually contemplating using the

25th amendment to remove the guy from presidency who the American people put there. We asked for him to be a witness and the Chairman said no. Instead we get 30 minutes from a guy who is going to prison for lying to Congress. Mr. Cohen, I have two quick questions for you: You were asked who all you talked to. You said Mr. Schiff, obviously Mr. Cummings. You're going before both committees. You're here today, you're going in front of Schiff's committee tomorrow. Have you spoken to Chairman Nadler or anyone on his staff? Or have any of your attorneys spoken to Mr. Nadler.

Cohen: I don't know about my attorneys. I have not spoken to congressman Nadler. I am not aware if my attorneys [have]. I can ask them.

Jordan: You can turn around and ask.

Cohen: The answer is no.

Jordan: You said at this time, Mr. Davis is not getting paid. Are you anticipating compensation in the future?

Cohen: When I start to earn a living.

Jordan: He's going to wait three years?

Cohen: The answer is yes.

Jordan: I've never heard of a lawyer waiting three years to get paid.

Cohen: I guess he thinks it is important.

Jordan: Wow. I yield to the gentleman from Arizona.

Gosar: Mr. Cohen, you are a disgraced lawyer. I mean you've been disbarred. I'm sure you remember, maybe you don't remember, duty of loyalty, duty of confidentiality, attorney-client privilege. I think the gentleman over your right side actually understands that very, very well and would aren't do what you are doing here today. So let's go back at this credibility. You want us to make sure that we think of you as a real philanthropic icon, that you're about justice, that you're the person that someone would call at 3:00 in the morning. No, they wouldn't. Not at all. We saw Mr. Comer dissect you right in front of this committee. You conflicted your testimony, sir. You're a pathological liar. You don't know truth from falsehood.

Cohen: Sir, I'm sorry. Are you referring to me or the President?

Gosar: Hey, this is my time.

Cohen: Are you referring to me, sir, or the President?

Gosar: When I ask a question, I'll ask for an answer. Now, are you familiar with rule 35 in the criminal rules and procedures?

Cohen: I am now.

Gosar: It is understood you've been in contact with the Southern District of New York. Is that true?

Cohen: I'm in constant contact with the Southern District of New York regarding ongoing investigations.

Gosar: Part of that application is to reduce sentencing time. Is it not?

Cohen: There is a possibility. . .

Gosar: The answer is yes.

Cohen: No, it is not.

Gosar: So testimony here could actually help you out and get your sentence lessened. Isn't that true?

Cohen: I'm not really sure how my appearance here today is providing substantial information that the Southern District of New York can use for the creation of a case. Now, if there is something this group can do for me, I would gladly welcome it.

Gosar: You know America is watching you. I've been getting texts right and left saying how can anybody listen to this pathological person. He's got a problem. He doesn't know fact from fiction. And that's what's sad here. You didn't do this for Donald Trump. You did it for you. This is all about you. The Twitter feed. Let me read another one: "Women who love and support Michael Cohen. Strong, pit bull, sex symbol, no nonsense, business-oriented, and ready to make a difference against the law." That is pretty sad. Over and over again, we wanted to have trust. It is built on the premise we are truthful. There is no truth with you whatsoever. That is why that is important that you look up here and remember the old adage our moms taught us: "Liar, liar, pants on fire." [Pointing to protest sign] No one should ever listen to you and give you credibility. It is sad. In fact, I want to quote the Chairman's very words: "This is a real sad state."

Cummings: Mr. Cooper.

Rep. Jim Cooper (D, Tennessee): Mr. Cohen, several times in your testimony, you state the bad things you did for Mr. Trump. And at some point, you apparently changed your course of action. There is a recurring refrain in your testimony that says, "And yet, I continued to work for him." At some point, you changed. What was the breaking point at which you decided to start telling the truth?

Cohen: There are several factors: Helsinki, Charlottesville, watching the daily destruction of our civility to one another, putting up silly things like this, really unbecoming of congress. That sort of behavior that I'm responsible for. I'm responsible for your silliness because I did the same thing you are doing now for ten years: I protected Mr. Trump for ten years. The fact that you pull up a news article that has no value to it, and you want to use that as the premise for discrediting me and say I'm not the person that people called at 3:00 in the morning, would make you inaccurate—in actuality would make you a liar. Which puts you into the same position I am in. and I can only warn people: the more people who follow Mr. Trump as I did blindly are going to suffer the same consequences that I'm suffering.

Cooper: What warning do you give young people who are tempted as you were? Would you encourage them not to wait ten years to see the light? What advice would you give young people, and, particularly, young lawyers, so they do not abuse their BAR license as you did.

Cohen: Look what happened to me. I had a wonderful life. I have a beautiful wife and two amazing children. I achieved financial success by the age of 39. I didn't have to go to work for Mr. Trump because I had to. I went to work for him because I wanted to. And I've lost it all. If I'm not a picture-perfect example of what not to do, that's the example I'm trying to set for my children. I've made mistakes in life and I've owned them. And I'm paying a huge price, as is my family. If that isn't enough to dissuade somebody from acting in the callous manner that I did, I'm not sure that person has any chance, very much like I'm in right now.

Cooper: A recurring theme in your testimony is the concern for your family's safety? What specifically are you most concerned about?

Cohen: The President . . . has over 60 million people. And when Mr. Trump turned around early in the campaign and said, "I can shoot somebody on fifth avenue and get away with it," I want to be very clear: He's not joking. He's telling you the truth. You don't know him; I do. I sat next to this man for ten years, and I watched his back. I'm the one who started the campaign. And I'm the one who continued in 2015 to promote him. There are so many things I thought he could do that are just great, and he can, and he is doing things that are great, but this destruction of our civility to one another is just out of control. And when he goes on Twitter, and he starts bringing in my in-laws, my parents, my wife, what does he think is going to happen? He's sending out the same message: He can do whatever he wants. This is his country. He's becoming an autocrat. And hopefully something bad will happen to me or my children or my wife, so that I will not be here and testify. That's what his hope was, to intimidate me. And I thanked everybody who joined and said that this is just not right.

Cooper: Have you seen Mr. Trump personally threaten people with physical harm?

Cohen: No. He would use others.

Cooper: He would hire other people to do that?

Cohen: I'm not sure he would have to hire them, they are already working there. Everybody's job at the Trump Organization was to protect Mr. Trump. Every day most of us knew we were coming in and we were going to lie for him on something. That became the norm. That is exactly what is happening right now in this country and that's exactly what's happening here in government, sir.

Cooper: Thank you, Mr. Chairman. My time is expired.

Cohen: Mr. Chairman, can we take a break?

RECESS

Rep. Virginia Foxx (R, Virginia): Thank you, Mr. Chairman. Mr. Cohen, you have admitted to lying on your taxes. According to federal prosecutors in the Southern District of New York, you also lied to banks to get loans. The prosecutors wrote quote "To secure loans, Cohen falsely understated the amount of debt he was carrying and omitted information for his personal financial statements to induce a bank to lend based on incomplete information," end quote. Is that correct?

Cohen: That's correct.

Foxx: You lied on financial documents. So, you lied to financial institutions in order to secure loans. So, we've established that you lie on your taxes, you to banks, and you have been convicted of lying to Congress. It seems to me that there's not much that you won't lie about when you stand to gain from it. In fact, the prosecutors for the Southern District of New York noted that each of your crimes quote "bear a common sense of characteristics which, each involving deception and being motivated by your personal greed and ambition." Is your appearance here today motivated by your desire to remain in the spotlight for your personal benefit?

Cohen: No ma'am.

Foxx: You have sought out ways to rehabilitate your image from tax evader, bank swindler and all-around liar to an honorable, truthful man by appearing before cable news. I'm concerned you could be using your story and this Congressional platform for your personal benefit, such as a desire to make money from book deals. So, can you commit it under oath that you have not and will not pursue a book or movie deal based on your experiences working for the President?

Cohen: No.

Foxx: You cannot commit to making money off of a book or movie deal based on your work.

Cohen: No, what I just—there's two parts to your question. The first part of your question, you asked me whether or not I had spoken to people regarding a possible book deal and I have, and I've spoken to people who have sought me out regarding a movie deal.

Foxx: No, I didn't ask you . . . I said, can you commit under oath that you will not, that you have not, and will not pursue a book deal.

Cohen: And I would not do that. No.

Foxx: Okay. Can you commit under oath that you will not pursue opportunities to provide commentary for a major news network based on your experiences working for the President?

Cohen: No.

Foxx: Can you commit under oath that you will not pursue political office in the State of New York?

Cohen: No.

Foxx: So, you don't commit to, uh, changing your ways, basically, because you want to continue to use your background as a liar, a cheater, a convicted liar to make money. That's what you want to do.

Cohen: And that's going to get me a book deal and a movie deal and television—a spot on television? I don't think so.

Foxx: Well, it appears that it will. I yield the remainder of my time, Mister Chairman to Mr. Jordan.

Jordan: I thank the gentlelady for yielding. Mr. Cohen, in your sentencing statement to the court and in December of last year you said, "I want to apologize to the people of the United States. You deserve to know the truth." Approximately a month later, Buzzfeed News ran a story that was *the* story in the country for a couple of days. Buzzfeed's story ran January 17th, 2019, on January 18th your counsel went on TV and wouldn't confirm or deny the story. The next day, the Special Counsel's office did something that's never happened, never happened. They said the description of specific statements to the special counsel's office and the characterization of documents and testimony obtained by this office regarding Michael Cohen's congressional testimony are not accurate. Why didn't your lawyer the day that he's on TV when this story is the biggest thing in the news and the country? Why didn't he deny the Buzzfeed story?

Cohen: Because I didn't think it was his responsibility to do that. We are not the fact checkers for Buzzfeed—

Jordan: He's on TV to talk about the very story you committed to the court when you were trying to get your sentence reduced that you—the American people deserve to know the truth. You had a golden opportunity to give them the truth on a false story, the Buzzfeed story, and your lawyer didn't say a thing. He acts . . . actually, he said this, "I can't confirm. I can't deny." You had an opportunity to do exactly what you told the judge you were going to do one month after you said it and you didn't do it. Why not?

Cohen: Again, it wasn't our responsibility to be the fact checker for the news agencies—

Jordan: This is the biggest story in the country—

Cohen: Sir, please, let me. . . .. The President says, so far, approximately nine thousand—

Jordan: Let me say one thing, I got eight seconds. I'll let you finish—

Cohen: Chairman, may I please finish—

Jordan: The Special Counsel said something they've never done. They said that story was false. Now you can respond.

Cohen: Okay. My response: the President has told something over 9,000 lies to date. Do I ask Mr. Davis or Mr. Monaco or do I go on television in order to correct his mistakes?

Jordan: When Mr. Davis—

Cohen: The answer, sir, is no.

Jordan: —on that specific subject, you should.

Cummings: Listen up. The gentleman's time has expired. You may finish answering the question and then we're going to go to Mr. Connolly.

Cohen: All I wanted to say is I just find it interesting, sir, that between yourself and your colleagues that not one question so far since I'm here has been asked about President Trump. That's actually why I thought I was coming today. Not to, not to confess the mistakes that I've made. I've already done that and I'll do it again every time you ask me about taxes or mistakes. Yes, I made my mistakes. I'll say it now again and I'm going to pay the ultimate price but I'm not here today and the American people don't care about my taxes. They want to know what it is that I know about Mr. Trump and not one question so far has been asked about Mr. Trump.

Cummings: Mr. Connolly.

Rep. Gerry Connolly (D, Virginia): Thank you, Mister Chairman. Well, Mr. Cohen, based on your testimony and your 10-year experience, um, I think you can recognize the behavior you're being subjected to on the other side of the aisle. Discredit, slander, uh, use any trick in the book to prevent your testimony from sticking. The idea that a witness would come to us who's flawed, and you certainly are flawed, means they can never tell the truth and there is no validity whatsoever to a single word would discredit every single criminal trial of organized crime in the history of the United States because all of them depend on someone who's turned. It would make RICO null and void. We couldn't use it anymore. This congress historically has relied on all kinds of shady figures who turned. One of the most famous who led to the decapitation of the organized crime families in America, Joe Valachi. Congressional hearing. He was a witness, and he committed a lot worse crimes than you're convicted of, Mr. Cohen. So, don't be fooled by what my friends on the other side of the aisle are trying to do today. It is do everything but focus on the principal, known as Individual Number One in the Southern District of New York, as I recall. Is that correct, Mr. Cohen?

Cohen: That is correct.

Connolly: Now, Mr. Cohen, I want to ask you about something that's not in your testimony and that so far it has not been made public. In our committee staff search of documents provided by the White House that were otherwise redacted or already in the public and I guess the White House thought that was funny . . . they made one mistake, the White House. There was an email from a special assistant to the President to a deputy White House counsel and the email is dated May 16th, 2017, and it says, and I quote "POTUS (meaning the President) requested a meeting on Thursday with Michael Cohen and Jay Sekulow. Any idea what this might be about?," end quote. Do you recall being asked to come to the White House on or around that time with Mr. Sekulow? May of 2017?

Cohen: Off the top of my head, sir, I don't, um. I recall being in the White House with Jay Sekulow and it was in regard to the, um, the documents, the document production as well as my appearance before the House Select Intel. But I'm not sure if that's specifically, but what I will do is I will check all my records and I'm more than happy to provide you with any documentation, uh, or, um, a response to this question.

Connolly: Well that's, you sort of touch on the, presumably the purpose of the discussion, at least among others. This occurred, this meeting occurred just before your testimony before the Select Committee on Intelligence here in the House. Is that correct?

Cohen: I believe so, yes.

Connolly: Was that a topic of conversation with the President himself?

Cohen: If this is the specific instance that I was there with Mr. Sekulow, yes.

Connolly: So, you had a conversation with the President of the United States about your impending testimony before the House Intelligence Committee. Is that correct?

Cohen: That's correct.

Connolly: What was the nature of that conversation?

Cohen: He wanted me to cooperate. He also wanted just to ensure, by making the statement, and I said it in my testimony, there is no Russia, there is no collusion. There is no, um, there is no deal. He goes, "It's all the witch hunt," and he goes, "This, this stuff has to end."

Connolly: Did you take those comments to be suggestive of what might flavor your testimony.

Cohen: Sir, he's been saying that to me for many, many months and at the end of the day I knew exactly what he wanted me to say.

Connolly: And why was Mr. Sekulow in the meeting?

Cohen: Because he was going to be representing Mr. Trump, um, going forward as one of his personal attorneys in this matter.

Connolly: So, it was sort of a hand-off meeting.

Cohen: Correct.

Connolly: Um, in any way—final question—did the President in any way, from your point of view, coach you in terms of how to respond to questions or the content of your testimony before a House committee.

Cohen: Again, it's difficult to answer because he doesn't tell you what he wants. What he does is, again, "Michael, there's no Russia, there's no collusion, there's no involvement, there's no interference." I know what he means because I've been around him for so long. So, if you're asking me whether or not that's the message, that's staying on point, that's the party line that he created that so many others are now touting? Yes. That's the message that he wanted to reinforce.

Cummings: Gentleman's time is expired. Mr. Massie.

Rep. Thomas Massie (R, Kentucky): Mr. Cohen, can you just clarify, did you say that at times you would do what you thought Mr. Trump wanted you to do, not specifically what he's told you to do.

Cohen: At times, yes.

Massie: So, you just went on your intuition.

Cohen: I don't know if I would call it intuition as much as I would just say my knowledge of what he wanted, because it happened before and I knew what he had wanted.

Massie: Does a lawyer have a duty to provide his client with good legal advice?

Cohen: Yes.

Massie: Were you a good lawyer to Mr. Trump?

Cohen: I believe so.

Massie: When you arranged the payment to Ms. Clifford, you say in your testimony, I'm going to quote from your testimony that you did so quote, "Without bothering to consider whether that was improper, much less, whether it was the right thing to do." You said that, unquote. That's your testimony today. You said you didn't even consider whether it was legal. How could you give your client legal advice when you're not even considering whether it's legal?

Cohen: I did what I knew Mr. Trump wanted. This conversation with Mr. Trump started—

Massie: I didn't ask where your good fixer. I asked whether you were a good lawyer.

Cohen: Yeah, well sometimes you have to meld both together. I needed to at that time ensure and protect Mr. Trump, and if I put my . . . which I'm clearly, clearly suffering the penalty of, I clearly err on the side of wrong.

Massie: So, you feel like by without bothering to consider whether it was proper, much less, whether it was the right thing to do . . . by ignoring any conscience, if you have one, that you were protecting Mr. Trump.

Cohen: I'm sorry, sir, I don't understand—

Massie: You feel that was how to protect . . . as his lawyer, you feel that you did a good job. You said you're a good lawyer, right? Is that being a good lawyer? To not even consider whether it's legal or not?

Cohen: I didn't work for the campaign. I was working, and I was trying to protect Mr. Trump. I sat with Mr. Trump and this goes back all the way to 2011—this wasn't the first scenario with Ms. Daniels.

Massie: Let's go back then.

Cohen: So, what my point, my point is . . . this is, this was an ongoing situation. It didn't just start in—

Massie: Right. Let's at least put—

Cohen: Please, you have to let me finish. Well, it started in, it didn't start in October. It started that many years earlier.

Massie: When were you disbarred?

Cohen: Yesterday, from what I read in the paper.

Massie: Yesterday. When should you have been disbarred based on the legal counsel you were giving your client?

Cohen: I don't have an answer for your question.

Massie: How long were you a counsel for Mr. Trump?

Cohen: Since 2007.

Massie: When is the first time you gave him bad legal advice or failed to inform him of his legal obligations . . . as you, as you testified today, you did in the case of the payment to Ms. Clifford. When was the first time you did that? Would that qualify for disbarment?

Cohen: I don't, I don't know, sir, I'm not the Bar Association.

Massie: I think you should consult with 'em maybe occasionally on some of these things.

Cohen: Well there's no point now. I lost my law license.

Massie: Has anybody, has anybody else promised to pay Mr. Davis for representing, you?

Cohen: No.

Massie: Nobody has.

Cohen: No. Are you offering?

Massie: Heh. Question quickly? Uh, July . . . you said, and this is also in your testimony, in the days before the Democratic convention, you became privy to a conversation that some of Hillary Clinton's emails would be leaked. Is that correct?

Cohen: Correct.

Massie: Okay. Was that in, you said late July? Do you know the exact day?

Cohen: I believe it was either the 18th or the 19th, and I would guess that it would be on the 19th.

Massie: But it was definitely July.

Cohen: I believe so, yes.

Massie: Do you know that was public knowledge in June. This was . . . Mr. Assange—and I'd like to submit this unanimous consent to submit this for the record—

Cummings: Without objection it's ordered.

Massie: Mr. Assange reported to the media on June 12th that those emails would be leaked. So, I'm not saying you have fake news. I'm saying you have old news and um, there's really not much to that. I would like to yield the remainder of my time to Mr. Higgins.

Rep. Clay Higgins (R, Louisiana): Thank you, sir. Mr. Cohen. I'm quoting you . . . earlier you said, "I spent last week looking through boxes to find documents" that would support your accusations. Where are those boxes, good sir. Where are those boxes? Are they in your garage or—

Cohen: They were in storage—

Higgins: And are these not boxes that should have been turned over to investigative authorities during the many criminal investigations you've been subject to?

Cohen: Sir, these are the boxes that were returned to me, post the raid?

Higgins: If they include data pertinent to crimes that you've committed, should they not have been turned over and remanded to investigative authority? Did Mr. Lanny Davis know of these boxes?

Cummings: Gentleman's time has expired. You may answer the question.

Cohen: I don't understand his question, sir.

Cummings: Very well . . . . Mr. Krishnamoorthi.

Rep. Raja Krishnamoorthi (D, Illinois): Mr. Cohen. Good morning. Thank you, Chairman Cummings for convening this hearing and thank you, Mr. Cohen, for voluntarily testifying this morning. Mr. Cohen, you were the executive vice president and special counsel for the Trump Organization, correct?

Cohen: I was the executive vice president and special counsel to Donald J. Trump.

Krishnamoorthi: And special counsel means you are the attorney for him. Is that right?

Cohen: It just means I was there in order to handle matters that he felt were significant and important to him, individually.

Krishnamoorthi: And those included legal matters?

Cohen: Yes, sir.

Krishnamoorthi: Sir, as a former attorney, you're familiar with legal documents known as nondisclosure agreements or NDAs, is that right?

Cohen: Yes.

Krishnamoorthi: Sir, I'm sure you know that NDAs properly written in scope can be reasonable in certain business contexts, but they can also be abused to create a chilling effect to silence people as we've seen in the #MeToo movement and other places. Isn't that right, Mr. Cohen?

Cohen: Yes.

Krishnamoorthi: And Mr. Cohen, the Trump Organization used NDAs extensively, isn't that right?

Cohen: That's correct.

Krishnamoorthi: Mr. Cohen, I'm reading from a recent *Washington Post* article regarding the language in one of these types of NDAs where the terms were described as "very broad." For instance, the terms "confidential information" was defined to be anything that quote "Mr. Trump insists remain private or confidential, including but not limited to any information with respect to the personal life, political affairs and/or business affairs of Mr. Trump or any

family member," close quote. Do those terms sound familiar to you?

Cohen: I've seen that document.

Krishnamoorthi: In fact, there's a class action lawsuit filed
this month by former Trump campaign worker Jessica Den-
son that this NDA language is illegal because it is too broad,
too vague, and would be used to retaliate against employees who complain of illegality or wrongdoing. Would you
agree that in the use of the ND—of these types of NDAs
with this type of language and later when Donald Trump
sought to enforce them, that he intended to prevent people
from coming forward with claims of wrongdoing?

Cohen: Yes.

Krishnamoorthi: Would you agree that the effect of the use
of these NDAs and their enforcement was to have a chilling
effect on people or silence them from coming forward?

Cohen: I apologize. I—If you want to define "chilling," I'm
not sure.

Krishnamoorthi: Oh, just, uh, that he would, in using these
NDAs or trying to enforce them would basically to keep
people silent.

Cohen: That was the goal.

Krishnamoorthi: And nothing at the Trump Organization
was ever done unless it was run through President Donald
Trump. Correct.?

Cohen: That's a hundred percent certain.

Krishnamoorthi: Okay. Mr. Cohen, do you believe that there are people out there today, either from the President's business or personal life who are not coming forward to tell their stories of wrongdoing because of the President's use of NDAs against them?

Cohen: I'm sorry, sir. I don't know the answer to that question.

Krishnamoorthi: Okay. Sir, I have a couple other questions for you. When was the last communication with President Trump or someone acting on his behalf?

Cohen: I don't have the specific date, but it was a while ago.

Krishnamoorthi: Okay. Do you, do you have a general timeframe?

Cohen: I would suspect it was, um, within two months post the raid of my, um, my home . . . hotel.

Krishnamoorthi: Okay, so early fall of last year, generally.

Cohen: Generally.

Krishnamoorthi: And what did he or his, uh, agent communicate to you?

Cohen: Unfortunately, this topic is actually something that's being investigated right now by the Southern District of New York. And I've been asked by them not to discuss it and not to talk about these issues.

Krishnamoorthi: Fair enough. Is there any other wrongdoing or illegal act that you are aware of regarding Donald Trump that we haven't yet discussed today?

Cohen: Yes. And again, those are part of the investigation that's currently being looked at by the Southern District of New York.

Krishnamoorthi: Sir, uh, Congressman Cooper asked you about, uh, whether you are, you are aware of any physical violence committed by President Trump. I just have a couple quick questions. Do you have any knowledge of President Trump abusing any controlled substances?

Cohen: I'm not aware of that, no.

Krishnamoorthi: Do you have any knowledge of President Trump being delinquent on any alimony or childcare payments?

Cohen: I'm unaware of any of that.

Krishnamoorthi: Do you have any knowledge of President Trump arranging any healthcare procedures for any women not in his family.

Cohen: I'm not aware of that. No.

Krishnamoorthi: Thank you. I yield back.

Cohen: Thank you.

Cummings: Mr. Cloud.

Rep. Michael Cloud (R, Texas): Thank you, Chairman. Mr. Cohen, can you tell me the significance of May 6?

Cohen: In terms of, sir?

Cloud: A couple months from now.

Cohen: That's the day that I need to surrender.

Cloud: Yes, sir—

Cohen: To federal prison.

Cloud: Uh, could you, for the record state, uh, what you've been convicted of?

Cohen: I've been convicted on five counts of tax evasion. There's one count of misrepresentation of documents to a bank. There's two counts, one dealing with campaign finance for Karen McDougal, one count of campaign finance violation for Stormy Daniels, as well as lying to Congress.

Cloud: Thank you. Uh, can you state what your official title with the campaign was?

Cohen: I did not have a campaign title.

Cloud: And your position in the Trump administration?

Cohen: I did not have one.

Cloud: Okay. In today's testimony you said that you were not looking to work in the White House. Uh, the Southern District of New York in their statement, their sentencing memo, says this, "Cohen's criminal violations in the federal election laws were also stirred, like others crimes, by his own ambition and greed. Cohen privately told friends, colleagues in including seized text messages that he expected to be given a prominent role in the new administration, and when that did not materialize, Cohen found a way to monetize his relationship and access with the President." So, uh, were they lying or were you lying today?

Cohen: I'm not saying it's a lie. I'm just saying it's not accurate. I did not want to go to the White House. I retained and I brought an attorney and I sat with Mr. Trump with him for well over an hour explaining the importance of having a personal attorney and that every President has had one in order to handle matters like the matters I was dealing with, which included some—

Cloud: I'll reclaim my time.

Cohen: Stormy Daniels. I was dealing with Stephanie Clifford and other personal matters that needed.

Cloud: Excuse me. This is my time. Thank you. Ask unanimous consent to submit the sentencing memo from the Southern District of New York for the record.

Cummings: Without objection. So ordered.

Cloud: All right, I'll get this to you in a second. Okay. This memo states that you committed four distinct federal crimes over a period of several years. You were motivated to do so by personal greed and repeatedly you used your power to influence for deceptive ends. It goes on to say that, uh, you were, that they each involved, they were distinct in their harms, but bear common set of characteristics, that they involve deception and we're each motivated by personal greed and ambition. Um, there's a lot we don't know in regards to this investigation, but here's what we do now: We know that you were expecting a job with the White House and didn't get it. You made millions lying about your close access to the President. You have a history of lying for personal gain, including . . . that's banks, about your accountant, to law enforcement, your family, to Congress, the American people . . . . At the Southern District of New York, you'd said that you did all this out of blind loyalty to Mr. Trump, but your sentencing memo states this: "This was not an act out of blind loyalty, as Cohen suggests. Cohen was driven by a desire to further ingratiate himself with a potential future President for whom his political set—success Cohen himself claimed credit for. Now we're in a search for truth. And I don't know, Chairman, how we're supposed to ascertain the truth in this quagmire of a hearing when the best witness we can bring before us has already been convicted of lying before us. And what's sad is the American people have seen this play out before. We have people in prominent positions fail and then a couple of years later they get a book deal. Now you're set to go to jail for a couple years. You come out with a multimillion book deal. That's, that's not bad living. And, uh, so my question is, is, will you, uh, today, will you today to commit to donate any further proceeds to book deals, to film reviews, to charity?

Cohen: No.

Cloud: Thank you. I yield—

Meadows: Will, will the gentleman yield?

Cohen: May I finish?

Cloud: Yield to Mr. Meadows.

Cohen: Mr. Chairman, may I finish? May I finish my—

Meadows: Mr. Cohen. He's yielded to me and so—

Cohen: I didn't finish, sir, my response.

Meadows: Listen, everything—

Cohen: Mr. Chairman, may I finish my response, please.

Cummings: I'll let you respond, but answer his question, please.

Meadows: Mr. Cohen, everything's been made of your lies in the past. I'm concerned about your lies today. Under, under your testimony, just a few minutes ago to me you indicated that you had contracts with foreign entities, and yet we have a Truth in Testimony Disclosure Form, which requires you to list those foreign contracts for the last two years, and you put N/A on there, and it's a criminal offense to not have that accurately. So, when, when were you lying? Either in the testimony to me earlier today or when you filled out the form?

Cummings: Gentleman's time has expired. Mr. Cohen, you may answer his question and then whatever you wanted to say on *his* questions.

Cohen: His questions, unfortunately, I don't have an answer for his question. But as was—

Meadows: No, no, no, no, no, no, no. Mr. Chairman—

Cohen: As it relates—

[gavel]

Cummings: The gentleman is out of order. I . . . he said he does not have an answer.

Meadows: Mr. Chairman, when, when we were in the majority—with all due respect, Mr. Chairman. Hold on.

Cummings: —to order. The gentleman has just said he doesn't have an answer and you have already over gone your time.

Meadows: And he's under oath to tell the truth. One of them is not accurate. Mr. Chairman—

Cummings: You will have time to answer a question.

[inaudible]

Cummings: Mr. Raskin. Mr. Raskin.

Rep. Jamie Raskin (D, Maryland): Mr. Cohen, thank you for your composure today. Our colleagues are not upset because you lied to Congress for the President. They're upset because you've stopped lying to Congress for the President. Now you've described the Trump campaign as a once-in-a-lifetime moneymaking opportunity, the greatest infomercial of all time, I think you said, and this may be the most trenchant observation of your whole testimony. Do you think the Trump campaign or Presidency ever stopped being about making money for the President, his family, and his organization?

Cohen: Yes.

Raskin: When did it stop being that?

Cohen: When he won the election.

Raskin: And what it become about at that point?

Cohen: Then it had to be about figuring out what to do here in Washington.

Raskin: Can you carefully explain to America how the hush money payments to Karen McDougal and Stormy Daniels worked? Can you carefully explain what catch-and-kill is?

Cohen: Sure. I received a phone call regarding both Karen McDougal as well as Stormy Daniels, obviously at different times, stating that there were issues that were going to be damaging to Mr. Trump. With the Stormy Daniels it started in 2011 when she wanted to have something removed from a website, and that was the first time I met Keith Davidson. I spoke with Keith Davidson, her then-acting attorney, and we were successful in having it taken down from the website. It wasn't until years later did—right, uh, by around the time of the campaign—did they come back and they ask what, what are you going to do now because she's back on the trail trying to sell the story. At which point in time, David Pecker on behalf of the *National Enquirer* reached out to her and her attorney in order to go take a look at, um, lie detector test that would prove that she was telling the truth. They then contacted me and told me that she was telling the truth, at which point, again all the time—

Raskin: She took a lie detector test—

Cohen: She allegedly took a lie detector test and was seen by an employee of the *National Enquirer*. At which point in time I went straight into Mr. Trump's office and I explained why this time it's different than another time.

Raskin: Okay. Now when you say different than another time, were there other women paid sexual hush money by Donald Trump or his organization? Was this a standard operating practice?

Cohen: No.

Raskin: So, you're not aware of any other cases where it had taken place?

Cohen: I'm not aware of any other case that Mr. Trump paid. So, which brings us to the Karen McDougal. He was supposed to pay. He was supposed to pay $125,000 for the life story of Karen McDougal. For whatever the reason may be, he elected not to pay it. David Pecker was very angry because there was also other monies that David had expended on his behalf. Unfortunately, David never got paid back for that either.

Raskin: So, David Pecker had done this in other cases of other mistresses or women?

Cohen: Other circum—circumstances, yes.

Raskin: Okay.

Cohen: Not all of them had to do with women.

Raskin: Are, are you aware of anything that the President has done at home or abroad that may have subjected him to or may subject him to extortion or blackmail?

Cohen: I am not, no.

Raskin: Okay. Um, are you aware of any video tapes that may be the subject of extortion or blackmail?

Cohen: I've heard about these tapes for a long time. I've had many people contact me over the years. Uh, I have no reason to believe that that tape exists.

Raskin: In December 2015, Donald Trump was asked about his relationship with Felix Sater, a convicted felon and real estate developer, and he replied, "Felix Sater, boy, have to even think about it. I'm not that familiar with him." Um, why did Trump endeavor to hide his relationship with Felix Sater and what was his relationship?

Cohen: Well, he certainly had a relationship. Felix was a partner in a company called Bayrock that was involved in the deal of the Trump SoHo hotel. Uh, as well as I believe the Trump Fort Lauderdale project. Why did he want to distance himself? That's what Mr. Trump does. He distances himself when things go bad for someone. And at that point in time it was going bad for Mr. Sater.

Raskin: You said you lied to Congress about Trump's negotiations to build his Moscow tower because he'd made it clear to you that he wanted you to lie. One of the reasons you knew this is because quote, "Mr. Trump's personal lawyers reviewed and edited my statement to Congress about the timing of the Moscow tower negotiations before I gave it." So, this is a pretty breathtaking claim. Uh, and I just want to get to the facts here. Um, which specific lawyers reviewed and edited your statement to Congress on the Moscow tower negotiations and did they make any changes to your statement?

Cohen: There were changes made, um, additions. Uh, Jay Sekulow, for one—

Raskin: Were there changes about the timing? The question—

Cummings: Gentleman's time has expired. You may answer that question.

Cohen: There were several changes that were made, including, um, how we were going to handle that message, which was—

Cummings: Mr. Cohen, are you finished?

Cohen: The message of course being the length of time that the Trump Tower Moscow project stayed and remained alive.

Raskin: That was one of the changes.

Cohen: Yes.

Cummings: Mr. Grothman.

Rep. Glenn Grothman (R, Wisconsin): Yeah. First of all, I'd like to clear up something, uh, just a little something that bothers me. Uh, you started off your testimony, you said it I think in response to some question that President Trump never expected to win. I just want to clarify that I dealt with President Trump several times as he was trying to get Wisconsin. He was always confident. He was working very hard, and this idea that somehow he was just running to raise his profile for some future adventure, at least in my experience, is preposterous. I, I always—I find it offensive when anti-Trump people imply that he just did this on a lark and didn't expect to win. But be that as it may, um, my first question concerns, uh, your relationship with the court. Um, do you expect, um, I mean right now I think you're, you're sentenced to three years, correct?

Cohen: That's correct.

Grothman: Do you expect anytime, uh, using this testimony, other testimony after you get done doing whatever you're going to do this week, do you ever expect to go back and ask for any sort of reduction in sentence?

Cohen: Yes. There are ongoing investigations currently being conducted that have nothing to do with this committee or Congress that I am assisting in, and it is for the benefit of a Rule 35 motion. Yes.

Grothman: So you expect, and perhaps what you testify here today will affect, going back and reducing this, what we think is a relatively light three-year sentence, do you expect to go back and ask for a further reduction?

Cohen: Based off of my appearance here today?

Grothman: Well, based upon whatever you do between now and your request for—

Cohen: The Rule 35 motion is in the complete hands of the Southern District of New York. And the way the Rule 35 motion works is what you're supposed to do is provide them with information that leads to ongoing investigations. I am currently working with them right now on several other issues of investigation that concerns them, that they're looking at. If those investigations become fruitful, then there is a possibility for a Rule 35 motion and I don't know what the benefit in terms of time would be, but this Congressional hearing today is not going to be the basis of a Rule 35 motion. I wish it was, but it's not.

Grothman: I'd like to yield some time to a Congressman Jordan.

Jordan: Yield to the gentleman from North Carolina.

Meadows: Mr. Cohen, I'm going to come back to the question I asked before with regards to your false statement that you submitted to Congress. On here it was very clear that it asks for contracts with foreign entities over the last two years. Have you had any foreign contract with foreign entities, whether it's Novartis or the Korean air line or Kazakhstan BTA Bank. Your testimony earlier said that you had contracts with them. In fact, you went into detail about—

Cohen: Sir, I believe it talks about lobbying. I did no lobbying. On top of that, they are not government—

Meadows: In your testimony—I'm, I'm not asking about lobbying, Mr. Cohen.

Cohen: They are not government agencies. They are private—They are privately or publicly traded companies.

Meadows: Do you have foreign contracts?

Cohen: I currently have no foreign contracts.

Meadows: Did you have foreign contracts over the last two years?

Cohen: Foreign contracts?

Meadows: Contracts with foreign entities. Did you have contracts?

Cohen: Yes.

Meadows: Yes. Why didn't you put them on the form? It says it's a criminal offense to not put them on this form for the last two years. Why did you not do that?

Cohen: Because those foreign, um, companies that you're referring to are not government companies.

Meadows: It says nongovernmental, Mr. Cohen. You signed it.

Cohen: They're talking about me as being nongovernment.

Meadows: And right, it says foreign agency. It says foreign contracts. Do you want us to read it to you?

Cohen: I read it and it was reviewed by my counsel, and I am a nongovernment employee. It was not lobbying and they are not foreign contracts.

Meadows: This has nothing to do with lobbying. It says it's a criminal offense to not list all your foreign contracts. That's what it says.

Cohen: Well, then I'm gonna to take a look at it before I leave and hopefully I will amend it prior to leaving because that's not the way I read your document.

Meadows: You know, it's just one more example, Mr. Cohen, of your skirting the truth. Okay. I want to ask one other question. So one other question, Mr. Cohen. It's my time not yours. Were you advised or was your counsel advise to withhold your written testimony to the latest possible date as John Dean said last night on CNN.

Cohen: Was it my what?

Meadows: Were you advised or was your counsel advised to withhold your written testimony to this committee at the latest possible date to get it to this committee at the latest possible date, as John Dean said that he advised you? Yes or no?

Cohen: No, we were working—John Dean? I've never spoken with John Dean.

Meadows: Has he spoken to your attorney?

Cohen: I don't know—I've never spoken with.

Meadows: Well, ask your attorney. He's right there behind you.

Cohen: We were working last night till eleven, twelve o'clock.

Meadows: You've known that you've been coming for some time. I—

[inaudible]

Cohen: We were working till eleven, twelve o'clock last night to finish everything.

Meadows: So, you writing it last night, Mr. Cohen? Don't give me that bull.

[gavel]

Cohen: We were making edits all the way through the night.

Cummings: Recognize Mr. Rouda.

Cohen: I'm sorry.

Rep. Harley Rouda (D, California): Thank you, Mr. Chairman. Mr. Cohen, in November 2013, President Donald Trump testified under oath in a lawsuit related to the failed real estate project, Trump International Hotel and Tower in Fort Lauderdale. During the deposition, President Trump was asked about his knowledge of Felix Sater, a Russian-born real estate developer and convicted member of the Russian Mafia, who according to press reports pled guilty for his role in a 40 million stock manipulation scheme. It is worth noting as well publicized the direct relationship between the Russian Mafia and the Kremlin.

Over the years, President Trump was asked how many times he interacted with convicted Russian Mobster Felix Sater. In 2013 President Trump testified that quote, "Not many. If he were sitting in the room right now, I really wouldn't know what he looked like," unquote. Mr. Cohen, as you previously testified, isn't it true that President Trump knew convicted Russian Mobster Felix Sater in 2013 when he made that statement?

Cohen: Yes.

Rouda: Isn't it true that because of Mr. Sater's relationship to the Trump Organization, that he had an office in the Trump Tower.

Cohen: And on the 26th floor, Mr. Trump—

Rouda: And the 26th four is important, why?

Cohen: Because it's Mr. Trump's floor.

Rouda: So, he had an office on the same floor as President Trump.

Cohen: In fact, his office, when he left, became my office.

Rouda: And isn't it also true that convicted Russian Mobster Sater even had business cards indicating that he was a senior adviser to Donald Trump as reported by the *Washington Post?*

Cohen: Yes.

Rouda: Did convicted Russian Mobster Sater pay rent for his office?

Cohen: No, he did not.

Rouda: So, based on those facts, isn't it true that President Trump misled at best, or worse, lied under oath?

Cohen: Yes.

Rouda: In December 2015, President Trump was asked again about his relationship to convicted Russian Mobster Mr. Sater by a reporter for the Associated Press. He stated, quote, "Felix Sater, boy, I have to even think about it," unquote. He added quote, "I'm not that familiar with him," unquote. Mr. Cohen, where would we find business records that explain the President's relationship to the convicted Russian Mobster Felix Sater. Would those be in the Trump Organization's files?

Cohen: They'd be in the Trump Organization's files. There would be cc's to Bayrock, which was the name of Mr. Sater's company. Um, I suspect on Mr. Sater's email address, possibly hard files in possession of Mr. Sater.

Rouda: And when you say in possession of the Trump Organization, where?

Cohen: It depends upon who the attorney was that was working on it. Now it would probably be, um, in a box, um, offsite. They have a storage facility that they put, uh, old files.

Rouda: In addi—In addition to convicted Russian mobster Sater, do you know of any other ties to convicted or alleged mobsters President Trump may have?

Cohen: I am not aware.

Rouda: Is it true that many people with ties to Russia ultimately bought condos and Trump properties, usually for cash? And if so, how many are we talking? 10, 20, 50?

Cohen: I'm not, honestly, sir, I'm not aware of any, um, you know, the statement that you're referring to, I believe it was made either Eric or Don and I don't agree with it.

Rouda: So, are you aware of any cash purchases by Russian oligarchs and family members of Trump properties?

Cohen: I'm not aware of that. I can tell you when you say cash, if you mean walking in with a satchel of rubles, the answer is I've never seen that happen. I've never heard of it. I will tell you when we sold Mr. Trump's property in Palm Beach, the home for $95 million, it came in by wire and that came from, um, Mr. Rybolovlev's bank account.

Rouda: One other question. You also talked about President Trump doing negotiations throughout the campaign regarding, uh, the Trump Tower in Moscow. Uh, was he directly involved in those negotiations? And if so, how do you know?

Cohen: Well, the answer is yes. And as it relates to negotiations, it was merely follow-ups as to what's currently happening, what, what's happening with Russia, meaning he wanted me to give him a status report. The problem with this is that the project never advanced because they were unable, Mr. Sater was unable to provide me with proof that somebody owned or controlled a piece of property that we can actually build on.

Cummings: Gentleman's time has expired. Mr. Amash

Rep. Justin Amash (R, Michigan): Mr. Cohen, uh, why did Mr. Trump choose to hire you and why did he trust you with the various tasks that you perform for him?

Cohen: I don't know, sir, you would have to ask him that question.

Amash: Well, uh, we've heard here that you have bad character. You've admitted to that over the years. You have no idea why he chose to hire you?

Cohen: In 2006 I was asked by Don, Jr. to come meet with his father. I did. He then followed up by asking if I would take a look at an issue that was occurring at Trump World Tower with the board. I went ahead and I looked into it and I found that the statements that the board were making about Mr. Trump were inaccurate. And the reason Don came to me is because I had an apartment there for investment. My parents had an apartment there. My in-laws lived there, friends of mine, we all bought as a big block from a brokerage company. We got a good price on each unit, and we ultimately turned over the board and I became actually the treasurer of the board because the out-of-control spending was going to put the building into bankruptcy. And I was proud to say that within a year we had plus $1 million versus minus one three. At the end of the day, Mr. Trump appreciated that and he tasked me with something else. It was to handle a problem that Don, Jr. had, um, created in terms of the business, a license deal. And we resolved that. And then on top of that, the third time Mr. Trump had asked me to take a look at the third Trump entertainment resort, um, Chapter 11 reorganization because he had a series of questions that he wanted answered. And I read these two stacked books, um, and gave him the answers that he needed and with that he, the next time I was sitting in his office and he asked me if I was happy at the sleepy old firm that I was with. I said yes. He said, would you rather work for me? And I asked him if he'd offer me a job. And he said, yeah. And we negotiated and I actually never went back to my office.

Amash: All right. You've suggested that the President sometimes communicates his wishes indirectly. For example, you said, quote, "Mr. Trump did not directly tell me the lie to Congress. That's not how he operates," end quote. Can you explain how he does this?

Cohen: Sure. It would be no different if I said, that's the nicest looking tie I've ever seen, isn't it? What are you gonna to, you gonna to fight with him. The answer is no. So you say, yeah, it's the nicest looking tie I've ever seen. That's how he speaks. He doesn't give you questions, he doesn't give you orders. He speaks in a code and I understand the code because I've been around him for a decade.

Amash: And it's your impression that others who worked for him understand the code as well.

Cohen: Most people, yes.

Amash: Mr. Cohen, I don't know whether we should, uh, believe you today, but I'm going to ask, uh, you this one last question. What is the truth that you know President Trump fears most?

Cohen: That's a tough question, sir. I don't, I don't, I don't have, I don't have an answer for that one. What does he fear most?

Amash: What's the truth that he fears most from your perspective? And again, I don't know whether we should believe you here today, but—

Cohen: It's, it's a tough question, sir. I don't know how to answer that question.

Amash: All right, let me ask you this. What principles have you chosen to follow in your life, and do you wish to follow different principles? Now?

Cohen: I've always tried to be a good person. I've tried to be a great friend. There were many, I think over 40 statements written in my support, uh, to the sentencing judge. I have friends who I treat incredibly well, that I know for over 40 years, and I treat people after 40 minutes the same exact way. Did I, am I perfect? No. Do I make mistakes?

Yes. Have I made mistakes? Absolutely. I'm going to pay the consequences for it, but all I would like to do is be able to get my life back, to protect my wife and my children, support, and grow old. That's pretty much where I'd like to be.

Amash: And you feel you're, you're following a different set of principles now than you followed throughout your life.

Cohen: I do. And I'm trying, I'm trying very hard. I thank you for your questions. Some of the other ones are really make it difficult to try to, you know, show some redemption. But you know, I am trying. I am trying.

Amash: Thank you.

Cohen: Thank you.

Cummings: Ms. Hill.

Rep. Katie Hill (D, California): Thank you Mr. Chairman. Uh, I want to mention really quick a clarification on the truth in testimony form. Uh, the mention was around whether it talks about foreign entities at all. And the question is, in fact whether witnesses have any contracts or payments originating with a foreign government. It does not cover all foreign entities, just foreign government entities. So, Mr. Cohen, what I'd like you, to ask you to do is review this issue over lunch with your attorneys. And if you need to amend your form, we ask that you do that before the conclusion of today's hearing. Also, I represent a purple district. I did not come here for partisan bickering. In fact, I actively wanted to avoid it. So, when I ask these questions today, it is not as someone who has a vendetta against the President. It's as someone who comes from generations of service members who swore an oath to obey the orders of the President of the United States and who along with myself and every single other person up here, swore to uphold and defend the Constitution of the United States. My forefathers served their country, they served their Commander in Chief, and they served the idea that America is free and just, and that the law of the land rules us all, especially those in the highest levels of our government. So, I ask these questions to help determine whether our very own President committed felony crimes while serving in the Oval Office, including efforts to conceal payments that were intended to mislead the public and influence the outcome of an election. I hope to God that is not the case. So, Mr. Cohen, on January 22nd, 2018, just days after the *Wall Street Journal* broke the story that Mr. Cohen paid $130,000 to Stephanie Clifford to silence her during the 2016 Presidential campaign, a nonprofit watchdog called Common Cause filed a complaint with the Department of Justice and the FEC alleging the payment to Ms. Clifford may have represented an illegal in-kind contribution to the Trump campaign. I ask that their complaint be entered into the record. On February 13th, 2018, Mr. Cohen, you sent a statement to the reporters that said, quote, "I used my own personal funds to facilitate a payment of $130,000 to Ms. Stephanie Clifford. And neither the Trump Organization nor the Trump campaign was party to the transaction with Ms.

Clifford and neither reimbursed me for the payment either directly or indirectly." Was the statement false?

Cohen: The statement is not false. I purposefully left out Mr. Trump individually from that statement.

Hill: Okay. Why did you say it that way?

Cohen: Because that's what was discussed to do between myself, Mr. Trump, and Allen Weisselberg.

Hill: So, it was carefully worded?

Cohen: Yes, ma'am.

Hill: Great. Mr. Cohen, a reporter, a reporter for the magazine *Vanity Fair* has reported that she interviewed you the very next day on February 14th, 2018, about the payment and reimbursement and she wrote quote, "Last February 14th I interviewed Cohen in his office about the statement he gave the FEC in which he said Trump didn't know about the Stormy payment or reimbursement for it." Do you recall this meeting with the reporter?

Cohen: I do.

Hill: The reporter also wrote, "Trump called while I was there. I couldn't hear much, but he wanted to go over what the public messaging would be." Is that accurate?

Cohen: It is.

Hill: Did the President call you while you were having a meeting with a reporter?

Cohen: Yes.

Hill: Did the President call you to coordinate on public messaging about the payments to Ms. Clifford in or around February 2018.

Cohen: Yes.

Hill: What did the President ask or suggest that you say about the payments or reimbursement?

Cohen: He was not knowledgeable of these reimbursements and he wasn't knowledgeable of my actions.

Hill: He asked you to say that?

Cohen: Yes, ma'am.

Hill: Great. And in addition to the personal check for $35,000 in July 2017, is there additional corroborating evidence that Mr. Trump, while a sitting President of the United States, directly reimbursed you hush money as part of a criminal scheme to violate campaign finance laws?

Cohen: There are 11 checks that I received for the year. Um, the reason why 11 was because, as I stated before, one had two checks.

Hill: And you have copies of all of those?

Cohen: I can get copies. I'd have to go to the bank.

Hill: So, we will be able to get copies of all 11 checks that Mr. Trump provided to you as part of this criminal scheme.

Cohen: It's either from his personal account as what was demonstrated in the exhibit, or it would come from the Donald J. Trump account. The, um, trust account.

Hill: Thank you, Mr. Cohen. I yield back the remainder of my time.

Cummings: Mr. Gibbs.

Rep. Bob Gibbs (R, Ohio): Thank you, Mr. Chairman. Uh, you know, I'm just from sitting here. I'm new to the committee. I'm not an attorney. Sometimes it seems your answers are incompetent or you are a liar. I think maybe I can be a better attorney. I don't know. Um, I'm looking through this. Uh, you come in here and you rail on the President of the United States, the Commander in Chief while he's over and across the Pacific Ocean trying to negotiate a deal to make this world safer. And Mister Chairman, just having this committee at this time when the Commander in Chief is out of this country, is just, is just, uh, I think is a new precedent. But you call him a racist, a cheat, and attacking his character, and I've been with the President a little bit. Uh, and, and, uh, I didn't see that in the President. I see a President who's very sincere, who's trying to make this country better for *every* American. And, and, and for you to come in here do that it's just a [inaudible] on your part. It's really unbelievable. Real repentance would be, go serve your time and, and, and, and, uh, don't, don't come back here and make allegations towards a man you can't substantiate. Now, I'm looking here from the, uh, remarks from the prosecutor of the Southern District of New York. Uh, false statements to Bank Three, which Cohen pleaded guilty "was far from an isolated event. It was one of the long series of self-serving lies Cohen told at numerous financial institutions." Earlier in your testimony, I think I heard you say that only there's a home equity loan. Apparently, the prosecutors in New York think that there was other financial things that you did. You also, they said, "managed to commit a series of crimes all withholding yourself out as a licensed attorney and upstanding member of the Bar." Um, also the Southern District, uh, prosecutors said that, uh, wrote that you're "consciousness of wrongdoing is fleeting, that your remorse is minimal and that your instinct to blame others is strong." Uh, so I'm kind of left here. Why you worked for the President for 10 years before he was President. If you have any sense of integrity that you're trying to tell us you have now, and it was that bad, why didn't you leave? You weren't, you weren't stuck there because of financial reasons. You had ways to leave. You're an attorney. Um, and so that's just kind of, you know, the President's working tirelessly and you're gonna make these allegations and you could have left anytime you want. It looks like to me you're trying to save face. And, and one of the other questions that came out here was, it looks like to me you're going to have a very, a lucrative deal at some point in your life, but you don't look like you're any closer to retirement. But you're gonna have some type of lucrative deal. And so one of my questions is, and it's come up a little bit, uh, talks with you and your attorney and there's been talks about members of Congress and staff and, and, and you said there was some discussions. Was any of those discussions that you or your attorneys had with members of Congress or staff or prosecutors, uh, to considerations to favor or other considerations to you or your family in the future?

Cohen: No, the conversations were about the topics and, uh, because there were things that originally we could not speak about at the request of—whether it was the special counsel's office or the Southern District or any of the other agencies, including the House Select Intel or the Senate Select Intel. Um, sir, just for your personal edification here, I was asked to come here. Um, your chairman sent a letter to Mr. Davis and I accepted. So, I'm here voluntarily.

Gibbs: Oh, I, I understand that—

Cohen: But if you believe that I'm here—

Gibbs: I understand that. I think this is political theater—

Cohen: Sir, if you believe—It's not political theater for me and I take no pleasure in saying anything negative about Mr. Trump. You've met him for a short period of time. I've been with him for over a decade. I've traveled with him internationally. I've spent dinners with him. It doesn't make me feel good about what's going on here. And as far as saving face, I'm not sure how being in front of the world being called a tax cheat—

Gibbs: Well, in this world today with these lucrative book deals, and movies that come about, I think you, you'll be pretty good in about five years. I yield the rest of my time to the Chairman [inaudible].

Rep. Jim Jordan (R, Ohio): I thank the gentleman for yielding. Earlier, you said you started the campaign.

Cohen: That's correct. In 2011.

Jordan: You started the campaign for President of the United States for Donald Trump?

Cohen: I certainly did, sir.

Jordan: Now that's news.

Cohen: ShouldTrumpRun.com.

Jordan: Wow.

Cohen: 2011. It was my idea. I saw a document in the newspaper that said, who would you vote for in 2012? Six percent of the people said—

Jordan: Michael Cohen, Michael Cohen—

Cohen: Six percent of the people turned around and said they'd vote for Donald Trump—

Jordan: The reason Donald Trump is President is because Michael Cohen started it—

Cohen: So, I brought it into his office. And I said to him, Mr. Trump, take a look at this, and he says, "Wow wouldn't that be great?" And with that is where it all started.

Jordan: Yeah. Okay. Like, I'm sure, I'm sure he had never thought of anything like that until you came along—

Cohen: No, I didn't say that he didn't think about it—

Jordan: Let me ask you one question. Look, I got eight seconds. I got eight seconds. Um, what did you talk to Mr. Schiff about?

Cohen: I spoke to Mr. Schiff about topics that we're going to be raised at the upcoming hearing.

Jordan: Whoa. [gavel] Not just what time to show up, actually what you're going to talk about?

Cummings: The gentleman's time has expired.

Jordan: Wow.

Cummings: Mr. Sarbanes. Mr. Sarbanes.

Rep. John Sarbanes (D, Maryland): Thank you, Mr. Chairman. Thank you, Mr. Cohen. I know the other side is suggesting that, um, you are an incorrigible liar and that you're lying here today. I can't think of anything you have to gain at this point from lying. I mean, they talk about book deals and other things that you want to do, but I see a lot more that you could lose, um, by telling the truth today, given the threats and other things that have been made against you and your family. So that's how I'm interpreting it. And, of course, you brought documents with you as well to bolster the credibility of your testimony. I did want to go back to an earlier line of questioning regarding the preparation, um, of your testimony before you came, before the intelligence committee. You talked about a meeting at the White House where the testimony was being reviewed, and I think you said that there was at least one White House attorney, Jay Sekulow, um, who was there and you acknowledge that there were some edits that were made to your testimony. Um, so on that topic, who at the White House reviewed your testimony?

Cohen: I don't, I don't know the answer to that. Um, the document was, was, um, originally created by myself, um, along with my attorney at the time, uh, from McDermott Will & Emery, and there was a joint defense agreement. So, the document circulated around, um, I believe it was also reviewed by Abbe Lowell, who represents Ivanka and Jared Kushner. Um . . . .

Sarbanes: Why did you provide, um, the testimony to the White House?

Cohen: It was pursuant to the joint defense agreement that we were all operating under.

Sarbanes: What were the edits that came back substantively on the testimony?

Cohen: I'm sorry, I don't know. Sorry. I'd have to take a look at the document.

Sarbanes: Did you, um, have a . . . Do you have a reaction to why there might not have been any sense of protest to what was gonna to be false testimony that was gonna to be provided to the Intelligence committee?

Cohen: No, sir, because goal was to stay on message. Was to just limit the relationship whatsoever with Russia. It was short. There's no Russian contacts, there's no Russian collusion, there's no Russian deals. That's, that's the message. That's the same message that existed well before my need to come and testify.

Sarbanes: So, it's an example of where this idea, this mentality of you toe the line, whatever the storyline or the narrative of the day or the month or the year is gonna be, you toe that line, whether it results in false testimony or not.

Cohen: I toed the party line and I'm now suffering and I'm gonna to continue to suffer for a while along with my family as a result of it. So yes.

Sarbanes: Let me switch gears quickly before my time expires. And you may not have direct knowledge of some of these things, but you're offering us some very helpful, uh, perspective on how the Trump world operates. And frankly, another reason I find your testimony fairly compelling and credible is because a lot of the things you're describing, a lot of the behavior described is very consistent with what we all see every single day. So, it's not, it's not a leap for us to arrive in the same place of perspective that you presented. Um, I'm interested in, in some of the activities around the Inaugural Committee, um, the inauguration of the President, there was an article, um, that appeared in, um, *Pro Publica*—it's a watchdog group—about some negotiation on pricing of things at the Trump Hotel where it looks like the, um, rental that was being quoted was substantially, even double what you would expect to pay according to what the market, uh, should bear. And, um, so in a sense the Trump Hotel was upcharging to the Inaugural Committee.

Cohen: Even I couldn't afford to stay there.

Sarbanes: Yeah. And so, I'm just curious, do you have a sense of whether that kind of a practice is something that is consistent or inconsistent? Is it possible that that kind of upcharging could be done inside a Trump operation?

Cohen: It did. It did happen—

Cummings: The gentlemen's time has expired.

Cohen: All I, all, what I can say to you is I wasn't part of the Inaugural Committee. Um, I raised a lot of money for the inauguration, but I was not part of it and there was a lot of, um, things, and that actually that issue is something that's also, obviously we've read about in the paper, being investigated at the current moment.

Sarbanes: Thank you.

Cummings: Mr. Higgins.

Rep. Clay Higgins (R, Louisiana): Thank you, Mr. Chairman. It's on my heart to tell you, sir, that I'm sorry for what your family is going through. I feel for your family. The Word tells us clearly that a man's mouth is his destruction and his lips are the snare of his soul. And I, I see you, a man trapped in that. However, I must tell you that I've arrested several thousand men, and you remind me of many of them, the ones that immediately become humble and remorseful at the time they're actually booked, and while they're incarcerated they're quite penitent and then return to their former selves when they're back on the street. So, respectful to your family and what they're going through, I owe you the honesty to tell you that that's my sense of you, good sir. I'm gonna give you another opportunity to respond to what you brushed off earlier regarding your own statement during this testimony from C-SPAN notation at two hours and 50 seconds in. You stated regarding your credibility that you're being accused of having no credibility. That is "exactly for that reason I spent the last week searching boxes to find the information that I did so that you don't have to take my word for it. I want you to look at the documents and make your own decisions." Now, the documents you're referring to, Mr. Cohen, are the documents that you submitted in your, with your testimony today, is that correct?

Cohen: That is correct.

Higgins: Do you believe they to be . . . those documents to be worthy of evidence for this oversight hearing today?

Cohen: I leave that to you to decide.

Higgins: And I ask you again, sir, and please don't be incredulous. This is a serious question. Where are those boxes that contain documents worthy of evidence to be presented to Congress and why have they not been turned over to investigating authorities looking into some of the many criminal activities that you're allegedly cooperating in? Where are these boxes? Who knows if these. . . Where is this treasure of evidence?

Cohen: The boxes that I'm referring to were boxes that were in my law office when the FBI entered and seized documents. When I was moving—

Higgins: Mr. Chairman, I would hope that the investigating authorities have noted what the gentleman had just stated and that actions be taken for those boxes to be seized and reviews based upon proper warrants signed by a sitting judge. You noted earlier today, Mr. Cohen, quiet incredulously to one of my colleagues who asked you regarding a television deal. Um, you expressed wonderment that your predicament could possibly get you on television. It certainly got you on television today, has it not, sir?

Cohen: Sir, I was on television representing Mr. Trump going back into 2011.

Higgins: Well, I didn't know you were until today really, until, until the FBI raided your home. Most of Americans didn't know who you were. How many attorneys you think Mr. Trump has had through the course of his career? Quite a few, I would imagine. You're, you're just one that's in a trap right now, and I understand you're trying to get out of it. You're in a bind, but I ask you, good sir, have you discussed film and book deals with, with your, your stated current attorney, Mr. Davis, Lanny Davis.

Cohen: With Mr. Davis? No. But I have been approached by many people who are looking to do book deals, movie deals and so on. And the answer to that is yes.

Higgins: That's your right as an American, but it, it, it leads me back to my instinct that compares you to many of the men that I've arrested during the course of my career. Mr. Chairman—

Cohen: With all due respect, sir.

Higgins: —I'm saddened that our, that our primary hearing to introduce the Oversight Committee of the 116th Congress to the American people has manifested in the way that it obviously is. This is an attempt to injure our President and lay some sort of soft cornerstone for future impeachment proceedings. This is the full intent of the majority. I yield my remaining 30 seconds to the ranking member.

Rep. Jim Jordan (R, Ohio): Mister Cohen, earlier you said the United States Southern District of New York is not accurate in that statement [pointing at screen].

Cohen: I'm sorry, say that again.

Jordan: Earlier you said that the United States Southern District of New York attorney's office, that statement is not accurate. You said it's not a lie. You said it's not accurate. You stand by that?

Cohen: Yes. I did not want a role in the new administration—

Jordan: So, the court's wrong?

Cohen: I, sir—Can I . . . Can I finish, please? I got exactly the role that I wanted. There is no shame in being personal attorney to the President. I got exactly what I wanted. I asked Mr. Trump for that job and he gave it to me.

Jordan: All, all I'm asking—and I appreciate it Mr. Chairman. You're saying that statement from the Southern District of New York attorneys is wrong.

Cohen: I'm saying I didn't write it and it's not accurate.

[gavel]

Jordan: All right. Thank you.

Cummings: Mr. Welch. Mr. Welch.

Rep. Peter Welch (D, Vermont): Uh, thank you. Uh, one of the most significant events in the last Presidential campaign, of course, was the dump of emails stolen from the Democratic National Committee, dumped by WikiLeaks. Mr. Cohen, during your opening statement . . . which was that at the height of the election you testified you were actually meeting with Donald Trump in July 2016 when Roger

Stone happened to call and tell him Mr. Trump that he had just spoken to Julian Assange. Is that correct?

Cohen: That is correct.

Welch: All right. And you said that Mr. Assange told Mr. Trump about an upcoming—I'm quoting your opening statement, quote, "massive dump of emails that would damage Hillary Clinton's campaign." So, I want to ask you about Roger Stone's phone call to the President. First of all, was that on speakerphone? Is that what you indicated?

Cohen: Yes. So, Mr. Trump has a black speaker phone that sits on his desk. He uses it quite often because with all of the number of phone calls he gets.

Welch: Now in January of this year, 2019, the *New York Times* asked President Trump if he ever spoke to Roger Stone about the stolen emails and President Trump answered. And I quote, "No, I didn't. I never did." Was that statement by President Trump true?

Cohen: No, it's not accurate.

Welch: And can you please describe for us to the best of your recollection—you were present—exactly what Mr. Stone said to Mr. Trump?

Cohen: It was a short conversation and he said, "Mr. Trump, I just wanted to let you know that I just got off the phone with Julian Assange and in a couple of days there's going to be a massive dump of emails that's going to severely hurt the Clinton campaign."

Welch: And was Mr. Trump and Mr. Stone aware of where those emails came from?

Cohen: Not that I'm not aware of.

Welch: Did Mr. Trump ever suggest then or later to call the FBI to report this breach?

Cohen: He never expressed that to me.

Welch: Did the President at that time or ever since in your knowledge, uh, indicate an awareness that this conduct was wrong?

Cohen: No.

Welch: The reason I ask is because on July 22nd on the eve of the Democratic Convention, WikiLeaks published, as you know, the 20,000 leaked internal DNC emails. Could your, uh, meeting with Mr. Trump have been before that date?

Cohen: Yes.

Welch: So, Mr. Trump was aware of the upcoming dump before it actually happened?

Cohen: Yes.

Welch: And is there any records—

Cohen: Though, sir, I don't know whether he knew or not, and I don't believe he did, what the sum and substance of the dump was going to be. Only that there was going to be a dump of emails.

Welch: And he was aware of that before the dump occurred?

Cohen: Yes, sir.

Welch: All right. And are there any records that would corroborate the day of this meeting? Calendars perhaps?

Cohen: I'm not in possession, but I believe again, this is part of the Special Counsel and they are probably best suited to corroborate that information.

Welch: Was anyone else present, uh, in the room during the call?

Cohen: I don't recall for this one, no sir.

Welch: Is there anyone else that the committee should talk to about the President's knowledge of the WikiLeaks email dump?

Cohen: Well, um, again, when he called, Rhona Graff yelled out to Mr. Trump, "Roger's on line one," which was regular practice.

Welch: And that's his assistant?

Cohen: That's, yes.

Welch: All right. And during a news conference on July 27th, 2016, then-candidate Trump public—publicly appealed to Russia to hack Hillary Clinton's emails and make them public. He stated, and I quote, "Russia, if you're listening, I hope you're able to find the 30,000 emails that are missing." Now, going back to Mr. Stone's phone call to the President, do you recall if Mr. Trump had knowledge of the WikiLeaks dump at the time of his direct appeal to Russia?

Cohen: I am not.

Welch: But the call with Mr. Stone you believe was before—

Cohen: Yes.

Welch: —the 27th.

Cohen: Yes, I'm, I'm sorry. You're—I thought you were talking about a different set of, um, documents that got dumped. So, I was in Mr. Trump's office was either July 18th or 19th and, yes, he went ahead. I don't know if the 35,000 or 30,000 emails, it was what he was referring to, but he certainly had knowledge.

Welch: All right, thank you. Just one last question. Uh, Mr. Raskin had been asking you some questions and one of the things in your answer was that Mr. Pecker, uh, expended other monies to protect, uh, Mr. Trump. Can you elaborate on what some of those other activities were?

Cohen: Sure. There was the story about Mr. Trump having a love child with an employee, um, with an employee. And actually the husband of that employee works for the company, as well. And there was an elevator operator who claims that he overheard the conversation taking place between one of Mr. Trump's other executives and somebody and he ended up paying like $15,000 in order to buy that story to find out whether it was true or not. And that's just one example of things that David had done over the years. It was the reason why in the recording when David was looking to become the CEO of *Time* magazine, we were concerned about, we'll call it the treasure trove of documents that had been created over the years, that if he left, somebody opened up the key to a drawer, find all this information. So, we were going to look to buy all of those life rights and so on.

Cummings: Gentlemen's time has expired. Mr. Norman.

Rep. Ralph Norman (R, South Carolina): Mr. Cohen, thank you for testifying. I join Mr. Higgins—Congressman Higgins in feeling for your family. They have no part in this. Uh, you know, I've heard all the testimony and I'm trying to decide what Clay's trying to decide, is, are you really, uh, sorry for what you did or he just got caught. And the thing that amazed me, uh, is that in your opening statement, uh, which let me quote, "Last fall I pled guilty in federal court to felonies for the benefit of at the direction of an in coordination with Individual One." Was that, uh, the President?

Cohen: Yes, sir.

Norman: Okay. Uh, your, your crimes were of your own to, to benefit yourself, uh, go through what you—

Cohen: Some of—Some of them, yes.

Norman: No, go through all the ones with the real estate, with the banks. Uh, on your HELOC Loan you failed to disclose more than $20 million in debt and you failed to disclose, uh, disclose 70,000 in monthly payments, um, on your fourteen-thousand—fourteen-million line of credit. You failed to disclose that you had drawn on that. So, this was all for yourself. This wasn't for the benefit of President Trump. This was to benefit Michael Cohen. So that's what—that's my question. Did you just get caught? Uh, and you worked for this man for 10 years, Mr. Cohen. You came in here with, with these, with these, uh, uh, he's a con man. He's a cheat. This is the very man that didn't you wiretap him illegally. Did you not wiretap President Trump without his knowledge?

Cohen: I did record Mr. Trump in a conversation. Yes.

Norman: Is that lawyer-client privilege, is that some . . . something that an honest guy would do? Honest lawyer?

Cohen: I actually never thought that this was going to be happening and that that recording even existed. I had forgotten.

Norman: But you did it.

Cohen: Yes, I did.

Norman: Have you ever, um—

Cohen: I had a reason for doing it.

Norman: What was your reason?

Cohen: Because I knew he wasn't going to pay that money and David Pecker had already chewed me out on multiple occasions regarding other monies that he expended.

Norman: But this is a man that you trusted. You'd take a bullet for. You secretly recorded. Let me ask you this, Mr. Cohen. Have you done, have you, uh, legally or illegally recorded other clients?

Cohen: I have recordings of people, yes.

Norman: Legally or illegally?

Cohen: I believe that they're legal.

Norman: Did you tell them?

Cohen: In New York State you don't have to do that.

Norman: So, you didn't tell him?

Cohen: No, I did not.

Norman: Okay.

Cohen: Sometimes I also used the recordings for contemporaneous note-taking instead of writing it down. I find it easier.

Norman: If the shoe were reversed, would you like, uh, your, your trusted lawyer recording you?

Cohen: I probably would not, no.

Norman: No, sir. It's, it's untrustworthy. It's something people just would not do. Now your bank loans that I just ran down, did you ever default on any of these loans?

Cohen: No, sir.

Norman: So the bank didn't take any loss?

Cohen: No. No. No bank has, I am not in default. I've never followed a bankruptcy. Um, the HELOC you're referring to? I replaced that from a different HELOC, paid it off. There is—I owe no banks any money.

Norman: How about your Medallion taxicabs today? Do you have to sell that?

Cohen: I'm still—well, the ones in Chicago, yes, I do have to sell. Um, however, um, in New York, the answer is no, I don't. And, um, they are, the industry is going through a major, major correction because of ride sharing. It's changed a lot of things.

Norman: The value of it has.

Cohen: Yes, sir.

Norman: Right. As the, uh, so no bank, will the banks make you loan again based on your record.

Cohen: Actually they did. They did. Post this—. Yes, um, the, the bank actually redid and they refinanced the entire package.

Norman: Currently.

Cohen: Post this—yes.

Norman: Okay. Have they ever had to do a loan loss reserve for the projected losses?

Cohen: I don't know what they did, but it's still the same amount. I didn't get the benefit of it. No, sir.

Norman: Most likely they did. I was on an audit committee.

Cohen: They may have—they may have done that, sir. But that's for their own banking. It—not from me.

Norman: No, it's by law. They have—if they suspect you of lying, which you have admitted to, if they suspect you have maybe not being able to make your loan payment, they have to have a loan loss reserve that's 125% of what you—if it's 20 million, they have to post in their account, uh, 20 million plus. So, they get no interest on it. You know who pays, who pays for that? The American public who deals with that bank?

Cohen: Yes, but, sir, I'm not in default and I'm current on each and every one of those Medallion loans. And I've never owed any money to First Republic Bank. In fact, at the time that I had the HELOC, I had more cash sitting in that same bank than, than the HELOC and my mortgage combined—

Norman: Last question—you're going over my time. Have you have been to Prague?

Cohen: I've never been to Prague.

Norman: Never have?

Cohen: I've never been to the Czech Republic.

Norman: Yield my, the balance of my time.

Cummings: Ms. Speier.

Rep. Jackie Speier (D, California): Thank you, Mr. Chairman. And thank you, Mr. Cohen. On page five of your statement, you say, and I quote, "You need to know that Mr. Trump's personal lawyers reviewed and edited my statement to Congress about the timing of the Moscow Tower negotiations." Who were those attorneys?

Cohen: Jay Sekulow—from the White House?

Speier: Yes.

Cohen: Jay Sekulow. I believe Abbe Lowell, as well.

Speier: And you have a copy of your original statement that you can provide to the committee?

Cohen: I can try to get that for you.

Speier: All right. If you would do though—do that. Um, the letter of intent for the Moscow Tower was in the fall of 2015, correct?

Cohen: Correct.

Speier: Uh, was there an expiration date on that of letter of intent?

Cohen: There was no expiration date.

Speier: So it could technically still be in effect today?

Cohen: No, it's been terminated.

Speier: It has been terminated?

Cohen: Yes ma'am.

Speier: Okay. Did Mr. Trump tell you to offer Vladimir Putin a free penthouse?

Cohen: No, ma'am. It was Felix Sater. It was a marketing stunt that he spoke about.

Speier: So Felix Sater had suggested to you that Mr. Trump offer a penthouse to Mr. Putin?

Cohen: Yes. Because it would certainly drive up the price per square foot. No different than in any condo where they start listing celebrities that live in the property.

Speier: In 2016 did you travel to Europe?

Cohen: Yes.

Speier: Did you meet with, um, persons associated with the Moscow Tower project?

Cohen: No.

Speier: It was for personal—

Cohen: Personal. My daughter was studying at Queen Mary in London.

Speier: So you did not meet with any Russians?

Cohen: No.

Speier: There is an elevator tape that has been referenced as a catch-and-kill product. Um, it was evidently of Mr.

Trump and a woman, presumably Mrs. Trump, is that correct?

Cohen: Are we talking about in Moscow or the, the Trump Tower elevator tape.

Speier: There's a, there's an elevator tape that went up for auction ostensibly in 2016.

Cohen: Yes. Yes, I've heard about this.

Speier: And who is on that tape?

Cohen: It's Mr. Trump with Melania.

Speier: And what happened in that tape?

Cohen: The story goes that he, um, uh, struck Melania while in that elevator because there's a camera inside, which I'm not so sure. Um, actually I'm certain it's not true. I've heard about that tape for years. I've known four or five different people, including folks from AMI, um, who have—

Speier: So, but there was some tape that went up for auction, correct?

Cohen: I don't believe that auction was real. And I don't believe anybody, I don't believe Mr. Trump ever struck Mrs. Trump ever, I don't believe it.

Speier: And are you aware of anyone purchasing that tape, then?

THE CONGRESSIONAL TESTIMONY [227]

Cohen: I don't believe it was ever purchased.

Speier: So, you never saw this tape?

Cohen: No, ma'am. And I know several people who went to go try to purchase it for catch-and kill-purpose. It doesn't exist. Mr. Trump would never do, in my opinion. That's not somehow—

Speier: Good to know. Good to know. Um, is there a love child?

Cohen: There is not to the best of my knowledge—

Speier: So, you would pay off someone to, uh, not report—

Cohen: It wasn't me. It was AMI. It was David Pecker.

Speier: So, he paid off someone about a love child that doesn't exist.

Cohen: Correct. It was about $15,000.

Speier: Okay. Um, how many times did Mr. Trump asks you to threaten an individual or entity on his behalf?

Cohen: Quite a few times.

Speier: 50 times?

Cohen: More.

Speier: 100 times.

Cohen: More.

Speier: 200 times.

Cohen: More.

Speier: 500 times.

Cohen: Probably. Over the, over the 10 years?

Speier: Over the 10 years, he asked you—

Cohen: And when you say threaten 'em, I'm talkin' about with litigation or an argument with, um—

Speier: Intimidation.

Cohen: A nasty reporter that has, is writing an article.

Speier: What do you know about, uh—let's go to your tapes. You said there's probably a hundred tapes?

Cohen: Voice recordings.

Speier: Voice recordings. And will you make them available to the committee?

Cohen: If you would really like them?

[Laughter throughout room.]

Speier: Did Mr. Trump tape conver—

Cohen: Don't you have to gavel that, sir?

Cummings: We would.

Cohen: Sorry.

Speier: Mr. Trump. Uh, did Mr. Trump tape any conversations?

Cohen: Not that I'm aware of, no.

Speier: Were you involved in the $25 million settlement to Trump University?

Cohen: I had, I had a role in that, yes.

Speier: Who paid the settlement?

Cohen: I believe it was Mr. Trump. I don't know the answer to that.

Speier: You don't know the answer, but you were involved in the—

Cohen: Yes, in a different aspect.

Speier: There's some reference to a businessman in Kansas being involved in that. Are you familiar with that?

Cohen: I'm not familiar with that, no.

Speier: All right. Finally, near my 13 seconds left, what do you want your children to know?

Cohen: That I'm sorry for everything and I'm sorry for the pain that I've caused them and um, I wish I can go back in time.

Speier: Thank you. I yield back.

Cummings: Gentlelady's time has expired. To the members of the committee, before we go to Ms. Miller for yours, so that you can properly plan, is a vote apparently coming up in about the 10 to 20 minutes. Uh, and what we will do is we will recess and we will come back, listen up, 30 minutes after the last vote begins. Got that? Not at the end. 30 minutes after it begins. And we'll do that promptly. All right. All right, Ms. Miller.

Rep. Carol Miller (R, West Virginia): I am very disappointed to have you in front of this committee today. Quite frankly, this isn't the reason the people of West Virginia sent me to Congress. I find this hearing not in the best interest of the American people. This is another political game with the sole purpose of discrediting the President. If it was not already obvious, there are members here with a singular goal in Congress to impeach the President. To achieve this goal, they will waste not only precious taxpayer dollars, but also time in this committee and Congress as a whole. In fact, they will go so far as to bring a convicted felon in front of our committee. We are supposed to take what you say Mr. Cohen, at this time, about President Trump, as the truth, but you're about to go to prison for lying. How can we believe anything you say? The answer is we can't.

This begs the question, why are those in the majority holding this hearing? I am appalled. We could be focused on actual issues that are facing America, like border security, neonatal abstinence syndrome, or improving our nation's crumbling infrastructure. Instead, the Democrats are trying to grasp at straws. Let's talk about this witness. From his sentencing hearing in the Southern District of New York, Judge Pauley stated, "Mr. Cohen pled guilty to a veritable smorgasbord of fraudulent conduct, willful tax evasion, making false statements to a financial institution, illegal campaign contributions and making false statements to Congress. Each of the crimes involved deception and each appears to have been motivated by personal greed and ambition." This is who we have in front of us today in our committee, someone who is about to be sent to prison for three years for evading his taxes, deceiving a financial institution, lying to Congress, among other accounts.

One of the most appalling facts about this hearing is that Mr. Cohen has used his experiences with President Trump both before and after he was elected for his own greed and profit. I'd like some yes or no answers. Isn't it true you tried to sell a book about your time with President Trump entitled *Trump Revolution: From the Tower to the White House, Understanding Donald J. Trump*?

Cohen: Yes. That happened early on when I was still even part, I believe, of the RNC.

Miller: And this book deal, which you had with Hachette Books, was worth around $500,000, isn't that correct?

Cohen: No, more, Ma'am.

Miller: How much more?

Cohen: It was about 750.

Miller: Wow. Mr. Cohen.

Cohen: I did turn it down.

Miller: Given that you continue to profit from publicly discussing your time with Mr. Trump, I worry that this committee hearing the majority has given you will only serve as a platform for you to continue to lie and sensationalize and exaggerate wherever it suits you. Do you plan to pursue another book deal about your experiences?

Cohen: Yes.

Miller: I would presume this book would be a little different than your latest past pitch, but your new angle might please some new fans. Anything to sell books. Mr. Chairman, we've canceled hearings on child separation and on other issues that are close to my heart for this media circus. What a waste of time and money. For a man who has gladly exploited the name of the President to promote his own name and fill his own pockets. It pains me that we are sitting here adding another chapter to his book. Thank you, and I yield the remainder of my time to Mr. Jordan.

Rep. Jim Jordan (R, Ohio): Thank the gentlelady for yielding. Earlier Mr. Cohen, um, uh, the gentlelady from California talked about this, um, this tape.

Cohen: I'm sorry sir, I can't hear you.

Jordan: Earlier, the gentlelady from California talked about this tape, this elevator tape that you said does not exist.

Cohen: That's correct. I do not believe it exists.

Jordan: But is it also your testimony that the Trump team was willing to pay to make sure a story about a nonexistent tape never became public?

Cohen: No, sir. That's not what, that's not what I said.

Jordan: They were willing to stop a false tape?

Cohen: We looked—we learned that this tape was potentially on the market and that it existed. And so what we did is exactly what we did with all the other catch and kill. We looked for it, and if in fact that it did exist, we would have tried to stop it. That's what I would have done.

Jordan: But it's a false tape.

Cohen: It's a false tape.

Jordan: Got it.

Cohen: I've never heard it, and I can assure you one thing about Mr. Trump, many things, he would never ever do something like that. I don't see it.

Cummings: Ms. Kelly.

Rep. Robin Kelly (D, Illinois): Thank you, Mr. Chairman. Mr. Cohen, I'd like to ask you more about the details of the $130,000 payment you made to Stephanie Clifford, the adult film actress known as Stormy Daniels, in order to purchase her silence shortly before the 2016 elections. First, according to documents filed by federal prosecutors in New York, you created a shell company called the Essential Consultants LLC. Is that correct?

Cohen: It's correct.

Kelly: And you created this company for the purpose of making the payment to Ms. Clifford, is that correct?

Cohen: Amongst other things, yes.

Kelly: You then use the home equity line of credit to fund the account in the name of Essential consultants LLC. Is that correct?

Cohen: That's correct.

Kelly: You then wired $130,000 to the attorney representing Ms. Clifford at that time and wrote in the memo field for the why and the word quote "retainer." Is that correct?

Cohen: Correct.

Kelly: Can you tell us why you decided to use this complicated process to make this payment?

Cohen: Well, starting an LLC is not a sophisticated means LLC. You call up a company, you pay for it, and they opened it for you. And the reason that I used the home equity line of credit as opposed to cash that I had in the same exact bank was I didn't want my wife to know about it, because she handles all of the banking, and I didn't want her coming to me and asking me what was the $130,000 for. And then I was going to be able to move money from one account to the other and to pay it off, because I didn't want to have to explain to her what that payment was about. I sent it to the IOLA account, the interest on the lawyers account to Keith Davidson, Ms. Daniels attorney—he would hold it in escrow until such time as I received the executed NDA, nondisclosure agreement.

Kelly: Did Mr. Trump know you were going through this process to hide the payment?

Cohen: Yes.

Kelly: Why not just use Mr. Trump's personal or company bank account to make the payment? Why was the distraction so important besides you not wanting your wife to know?

Cohen: What his concern was, was that there would be a check that has his very distinct signature onto it. And even after she cashed the check, all you need to do is make a photocopy of it, and it's kind of proof positive on exactly what took place. So here he—the goal was to keep him far away from it as possible.

Kelly: Can anyone corroborate what you have shared with us?

Cohen: Absolutely.

Kelly: And that is?

Cohen: Keith Davidson. Allen Weisselberg. President Trump.

Kelly: Okay. Now let's talk about the reimbursement. According to federal prosecutors, and I quote, "After the election, Cohen sought reimbursement for a lecture and related expenses, including the $130,000 payment." Prosecutors stated that you, and I quote, "presented an executive—an executive of the company with a copy of a bank statement reflecting the $130,000 wire transfer." Is that accurate?

Cohen: That is accurate.

Kelly: Do you still have a copy of that bank statement?

Cohen: Yes. It's actually made part of the exhibit.

Kelly: Okay, so you will provide it to the committee?

Cohen: Yes, ma'am.

Kelly: According to federal prosecutors, executives at the company then, and I quote, "agreed to reimburse Cohen by adding 130,000 and 50,000 grossing up that amount to

360,000 for tax purposes and adding a $60,000 bonus such that Cohen would be paid 420,000 in total. Executives of the company decided to pay the 420,000 in monthly install-ments at 35,000 over the course of a year." Is that accurate?

Cohen: That is accurate.

Kelly: What was the purpose of grossing up, the amounts, essentially doubling what you had paid to Ms. Clifford and others?

Cohen: Because if you pay $130,000 and you live in New York where you have a 50% tax bracket, um, in order to get you 130 back, you have to have 260. Otherwise, my wife—if he gave me back 130, I would only—then I'd be out $65,000.

Kelly: What was the purpose of spreading the reimburse-ments to you over the 12 monthly installments?

Cohen: That was in order to hide what the payment was. I obviously wanted the money in one shot. I would've pre-ferred it that way, but in order to be able to, um, put it onto the books, Allen Weisselberg made the decision that it should be paid over the 12 months so that it would look like a retainer.

Kelly: And did Mr. Trump know about this, uh, reimburse-ment method?

Cohen: Oh, he knew about everything. Yes.

Kelly: Okay. Well thank you Mr. Cohen. So the President not only knew about the payments, he knew and helped to hide the payments and the reimbursements to you.

Cohen: We discussed it. Everything had to go through Mr. Trump, and it had to be approved by Mr. Trump.

Kelly: And now you're going to prison and he's in the White House.

Cohen: And I'm going to prison, yes ma'am.

Kelly: I yield back.

Cummings: Mr. Armstrong.

Rep. Kelly Armstrong (R, North Dakota): Thank you, Mr. Chairman. Uh, earlier. Yeah.

Kelly: Yes, I yield my time.

Armstrong: Earlier you'd said—I'm assuming New York's a one party consent state, one person can record the other one without it being illegal?

Cohen: Correct.

Armstrong: But you also were a member of the New York bar?

Cohen: I was, yes.

Armstrong: How would you rate recording clients in the ethical realm of being a lawyer?

Cohen: It's not illegal and—

Armstrong: I'm not asking if it's illegal, I'm asking if it's ethical.

Cohen: I don't, I don't know.

Armstrong: Okay.

Cohen: We'd have to leave that judgment to the Bar Association.

Armstrong: Well, I think every other lawyer in here knows exactly where it is on the ethical standard. Um, when you said you had a hundred tapes, were any of those tapes of other clients?

Cohen: Yes.

Armstrong: And—I think this is pretty amazing. I really do. Did any of them waive privilege?

Cohen: No.

Armstrong: So five minutes ago in the middle of our hearing on oversight, you just immediately responded that you would you would hand over tapes to this committee without any of your previous clients waiving privilege.

Cohen: I'm not the only one in possession of those documents. Those documents were in the hands of all of the agencies—

Armstrong: Whoever else is in charge of those documents is not my concern. My concern is I know lawyers that would go to jail before they would violate attorney client privilege, and in a manner of a second you just said, "Absolutely, I will turn those over."

Cohen: Just trying to cooperate, sir.

Armstrong: At the expense of clients who have never waived privilege.

Cohen: They're already in the hands, sir, of all of the agencies as was—I didn't ask people—

Armstrong: What law enforcement determines to do with something and what you determine to do as something— client privilege and attorney trust accounts are about the two most sacred things that you can ever do in your entire career as a lawyer.

Cohen: And, and by the way, sir—

Armstrong: And in the matter of a second—

Cohen: And the tape with Mr. Trump—

Armstrong: Completely—

Cohen: The reason that it's out there is because Rudy Giuliani waived the proof.

Armstrong: I'm not talking about Rudy Giuliani, I'm talking about you in a ma—this is, I don't know who's on those tapes. Only you know who is on those tapes. There are hundreds of them.

Cohen: The other one is also subject an ongoing investigation.

Armstrong: My point is within a matter of a second, one second, you took no, absolutely no calculation of your role as those clients counselor, the role that plays in privacy and in the role that plays in a solemn vow you took when you pass the bar, when you signed onto the bar until recently, were a member of the bar, and you just immediately said, "If it—if it helps me out in the two day in front of TV, yes, absolutely Mr. Chairman, you can have that." And I think and that just goes into what we're going to talk about next, briefly. We talk about these tax—these indictments on tax fraud and bank fraud as if they are isolated incidents, but they're not isolated incidents of bad judgment. These were intricate, elaborate lies that created—that needed to be held with constant miss—I mean just constant deceptions of banks, businesses, associates, accountants, potentially your family. Um, you received over 2.4 million in personal loans from taxi company, taxi, medallion company one. And those were loan payments for a business loan, correct?

Cohen: No sir, they—

Armstrong: You weren't receiving—

Cohen: Those—

Armstrong: Okay, go ahead.

Cohen: Those were payments that were made by the management company that was operating the medallions.

Armstrong: To you.

Cohen: To me.

Armstrong: So, and those were just—those were deposited into your personal account and in some instances your wife's account?

Cohen: It was, it was deposited into the joint checking account of my wife and I that's located at the base of the building that we resided.

Armstrong: And were those disclosed on your tax returns?

Cohen: They are not, they were not disclosed on my tax return.

Armstrong: And in fact, when your accountants talked to you about those, those deposits, you told them you wouldn't pay for a memo that you didn't ask to be done?

Cohen: That's inaccurate.

Armstrong: So the sentencing court in New York has that wrong.

Cohen: Okay. Um, I don't know what Mr. Getzel wrote—my accountant—um, there are series of issues regarding his memo, anyway, including the fact he's almost directed me in an earlier memo to commit fraud. But putting all that aside with Jeff Getzel, um, the answer to that is I pled guilty. All right? And I made my mistake and I'm going, as I've said a hundred times now, right? I'm not so sure why the singular attack on my taxes. If you want to look at them, I'm more than happy to show them to you, but every single word—

Armstrong: If the Chairman will give me 20 minutes, I got plenty of other things to talk about—

Cohen: Every single word that's written about me is not 100% accurate.

Armstrong: All right, I'm going to reclaim my time.

Cohen: And that's exactly why when it comes to the credibility, why I asked Mr. Davis, Mr. Monaco to please, let's figure out how—

Armstrong: But that's my point with the credibility—

Cohen: You understand—

Armstrong: These aren't isolated—

Cohen: The credibility that I'm trying—

Armstrong: These are not isolated incidents of attack. These were constant deceptions. Whether it's rolling over a $20 million line of credit to a $14 million credit. You went through great lengths to conceal that from one bank while at the same time, you are reducing your net income to another bank. These aren't things that happened on January 1 of '18, January 1 of '17, January 1 of '15, these are things that were constantly involved on a—My question is, was it exhausting keeping track of all the lies you were telling all these people?

Cummings: The gentleman's time has expired.

Cohen: I don't have an answer for him.

Cummings: Very well. Mr. DeSaulnier—

Cohen: I just thank you for continuing the narrative.

Rep. Mark DeSaulnier (D, California): Thank you Mr. Chairman. Mr. Cohen. Good luck on your road to redemption.

Cohen: Thank you. It's going to be a long way.

DeSaulnier: Now the opposite of that is perdition, as I remember, and that's particularly hard on your children, so I wish you well and I wish your family well. Mr. Cohen, as you sort of describe your road to here, Mr. Cooper asked you where, when the moment was, or moments when you decided you needed to change, it strikes me there is a transition that you have, you have illuminated here; your period of time, the 10 years working for somebody who you admired as a developer, and then when Charlottesville happened, and quite frankly, uh, when the special counsel called you, called you in obviously was a key part of it or you wouldn't be here. Um, but the in-between part I find really interesting and troubling at least in terms of appearances and confidence that the American people would have in this institution and, and democracy quite frankly.

So during that period of time, I want to ask you about two specific, if we have enough time. First, uh, the Trump Tower. So you were negotiating for this, as you said, it was to be the tallest building in Europe. Um, in your guilty plea with the special counsel, you quote, say, it quotes, "Cohen asked Individual 1. . ." Is that President Trump?

Cohen: Yes.

DeSaulnier: Okay. ". . .about the possibility of President Trump traveling to Russia in connection with the Moscow project and asked a senior campaign official about potential businesses travel, business travel to Russia." Uh, what, when did this conversation happen, do you recall?

Cohen: Early on in the campaign.

DeSaulnier: And who was the campaign official?

Cohen: Corey Lewandowski.

DeSaulnier: What, what did you discuss in this meeting?

Cohen: Possibility of which dates that Mr. Trump would have availability if in fact that we were going to go over to

Russia to take a look at the project when the porch—I'm sorry sir?

DeSaulnier: Go ahead.

Cohen: Um, unfortunately, it never came to fruition because we were never successful in getting the first prong of what I needed, which was ownership or control over a piece of property. And until such time, there was no reason to come up with a date. But when I first received the information request to go to Russia, what I decided to do is, I spoke to Mr. Trump about it. He told me to speak to Corey and see what dates might be available if I got the information I needed.

DeSaulnier: So it stopped because of appearances or, or did it stop because the parties decided not to pursue it?

Cohen: I'm so sorry, I don't understand your question.

DeSaulnier: So why did the pursuit of the Trump Tower that Mr. Trump has now said, of course he pursued it because he thought he might be going back into the development business. Why was the reason that the deal stopped?

Cohen: Because he won the Presidency?

DeSaulnier: Okay, so in that interim period of time, you must admit it looks troubling that now that we know what foreign influence was attempting to do, whether there was collusion or not, it certainly appears troubling that you were—Mr. Trump was part of this negotiation and at the same time, what we know, perhaps separately, that the Russians were engaged in our election.

Cohen: Well, I don't know about them being engaged in the election. I can only talk for myself here. I would say to Mr. Trump in response to his question, "What's going on with Russia?" is "I'm still waiting for documents," and then that night at a rally, he would turn around and do his battle cry of, "No Russia, No collusion, No involvement, Witch Hunt."

DeSaulnier: Okay. On a separate subject, but somewhat related. On January 17 of this year, the *Wall Street Journal* published a story stating that you hire John Gauger, the owner of a consulting company who works for Liberty University in Virginia, to rig at least two online polls related to Donald Trump. Did you hire him?

Cohen: Those were back, um, in I believe 2015.

DeSaulnier: 2014.

Cohen: 2014.

DeSaulnier: So you did hire him?

Cohen: Yes. I spoke with Mr. Gauger about manipulating these online polls.

DeSaulnier: And did he use bots to manipulate the poll?

Cohen: He used algorithms and if that includes bots than the answer is yes.

DeSaulnier: Yes, that's accurate. Did the President have any involvement?

Cohen: Yes.

DeSaulnier: In directing you to do this?

Cohen: Yes.

DeSaulnier: What were the results of that poll?

Cohen: Exactly where we wanted them to be in the CNBC poll, we came in at number nine and the Drudge Report, he was top of the Drudge Report as well.

DeSaulnier: Okay.

Cohen: Poll. And please understand, so the CNBC poll was called The Contenders and it was top 250 people that they named and it was supposed to be the top 10 most influential piece.

DeSaulnier: Let me just finish with earlier today, you directed a comment to my colleagues—and I'm quoting so correct me if I got this wrong—you said, "The more people who follow Mr. Trump, the more people will be where I am." Is it your expectation that people in the administration will end up where you are?

Cohen: Sadly, if they follow blind—blindly like I have, I think the answer is yes.

Cummings: Thank you.

Cummings: You time has expired, Mr. Steube.

Rep. Greg Steube (R, Florida): Thank you, Mr. Chairman. Uh, when I ran for Congress I talked about how Washington was broken, but I certainly did not expect the level of political gamesmanship and partisanship and sheer stagnation of policies that would improve the lives of Americans that I'm a witnessing today. It is terribly disappointing to me that this committee and its chairman chose to spend our time in questioning an individual that has zero probative value and zero credibility, instead of spending our limited time focusing on improving the lives of Americans, creating jobs or streamlining the functioning of our federal government. Yet here we are, taking testimony from a convicted liar and not someone who has just lied to his clients or family or friends, but testimony from an individual who deliberately and premeditatedly lied to this body. He lied to Congress through false statements and written statements. He lied to Congress through his testimony. He then amplified his false statements by releasing and repeating his lies to the public, including the other potential witnesses. Yet now we on this committee and the American people are expected to believe Mr. Cohen's testimony. I don't know a juror in America that would believe anything Mr. Cohen says, given his past actions and lies. Mr. Cohen, you stood before multiple Congressional committees before today and raised your right hand and swore an oath, to be honest. Is that correct?

Cohen: That is correct.

Steube: And you lied to those Congressional committees, is that correct?

Cohen: Previously?

Steube: Correct.

Cohen: Yes, sir.

Steube: You stated that Trump never directed you to lie to Congress. Is that correct?

Cohen: That's correct.

Steube: Therefore, you lied to Congress on your own accord and then admitted to lying to Congress. Correct?

Cohen: I've, I've already stated my peace on that. I knew what he wanted me to do. I was staying on party line.

Steube: But he never directed you to lie to Congress.

Cohen: He did not use those words, no.

Steube: In your evidence that you provided this committee a mere two hours before the hearing started, were payments made to you by Mr. Trump, correct?

Cohen: Amongst other things, yes.

Steube: Yet, other than your testimony here today, there's absolutely no proof that those specific payments were for those specific purposes. Is that correct?

Cohen: It's my testimony that the check that I produced as part of this testimony, the 35,000 and then the second check that's signed by Allen Weisselberg and Don Trump Jr. were two checks out of the 11 that were meant for the reimbursement of the hush money payment to Stormy Daniels.

Steube: So in your testimony on page 13 you claim, and I quote, "Mr. Trump directed me to use my own personal funds from a home equity line of credit to avoid any money being tracked back to him that could negatively impact his campaign." Do you have any proof of this direction?

Cohen: Just the payment, sir.

Steube: So no email.

Cohen: Mr. Trump doesn't have email.

Steube: So no recording.

Cohen: I do not have recordings, no.

Steube: No text message.

Cohen: Mr. Trump doesn't text message.

Steube: So no direction other than your testimony today that that's what the payment was for.

Cohen: And the fact that I paid on his behalf, at his direction, the money to Keith Davidson's IOLA account. You're right. There's no other tes—there's no other documentation I have.

Steube: So nothing that you produce as part of your exhibits proved that President Trump directed you in any way to make that payment?

Cohen: I don't even know how to answer that, sir.

Steube: Well, it's, it's pretty simple. There's nothing in the evidence that shows that the exhibits that you provided today, that show that Trump directed you to make those payments

Cohen: Other than the nondisclosure agreement that has been seized by government authorities and is widely shown. I don't believe there's anybody out there that believes that I just decided to pay $130,000 on his behalf.

Steube: Well you were, you were his attorney for over 10 years.

Cohen: That doesn't mean that I pay $130,000.

Steube: Well, it doesn't mean that he wasn't paying you for representation of counsel.

Cohen: Okay.

Steube: So how did President Trump even knew you had a HELOC?

Cohen: I'm so sorry sir?

Steube: How did President Trump even know you had a HELOC?

Cohen: Because we discussed it. Because I told him the same thing, that I didn't want my wife to find out about it. And as one additional—Rudy Giuliani himself came out and expressed that Mr. Trump reimburse me for the, for the money that was spent to pay Stormy Daniels.

Steube: And did you tell Chris Cuomo that you had no access to Mr. Trump during October and November of 2016?

Cohen: I'm sorry, I don't know what you're referring to.

Steube: Your interview with Chris Cuomo.

Cohen: I would need to see the document. I—

Steube: Oh, did you also tell Chris Cuomo that you made these payments without telling Mr. Trump because you wanted to protect Mr. Trump?

Cohen: And I was protecting Mr. Trump.

Steube: And you told him that you made these payments without telling him.

Cohen: When I said that—if that's what I said to Chris Cuomo, yes. That was my, that was my line.

Steube: And if this unsupported claim was true, then it would be part of an ongoing investigation as evidence of a crime and the Department of Justice would not let you discuss it during your testimony here today. Is that correct?

Cohen: I don't know.

Cummings: Time is expired. Did you answer?

Cohen: Yes. I, I did want to say one last thing. Not only did I lie to the American people, I lied to the First Lady when the President called me and I was sitting in a car with a friend of mine, and he had me speak to her and explain to the First Lady. So the answer is they're—you're—you're not accurate. And I don't feel good about any of this. And this was not my intention.

Cummings: Ms. Lawrence.

Cohen: Sorry.

Rep. Brenda Lawrence (D, Michigan): Thank you, Mr. Chairman. Um, I just want to put it on the record as being a black American and having endured the public comments of racism from the sitting President as being a black person, I can only imagine what's being said in private. And to prop up one member of our entire race, of black people, and say that that nullifies, that is totally insulting and in, in, in this environment of expecting a President to be inclusive and to look at his administration speaks volumes. So I have some questions.

I want to talk to you about this intimidation of witness. Mr. Cohen, you were initially scheduled to testify before the House Oversight Committee on February the 7th, but your legal team delayed your testimony quoting ongoing threats against your family from the President and Attorney Giuliani. Is that correct?

Cohen: Yes, ma'am.

Lawrence: And then on November 29th, after you admitted that the President's negotiations over a real-estate project in Russia continued well through the summer before the 2016 election, President Trump called you quote, "a weak person" and accused you of lying. And then on December 16, 2018, after you disclosed that it was the President who directed you to arrange hush money payment to Stormy Daniels and Karen McDougal to conceal his extramarital affairs, he called you—the President of the United States—a rat. Mr. Cohen, why do you feel or believe that the President is repeatedly attacking you? You are stating that you feel intimidated asking us to protect you following your cooperation with law enforcement.

Cohen: When you have access to 60 plus million people that follow you on social media, and you have the ability

within which to spark some action by individuals that follow—that follow him, and from his own words that he can
walk down Fifth Avenue, shoot someone and get away with
it. It's never comfortable when the President of the United
States—

Lawrence: What do you think he can do to you?

Cohen: A lot. And it's not just him. It's those people that
follow him in his rhetoric.

Lawrence: What is a lot?

Cohen: I don't know. I don't walk with my wife if we go to a
restaurant or we go somewhere, I don't walk with my children. I make them go before me because I'm—I have fear,
and it's the same fear that I had before when he initially
decided to drop that tweet in my cell phone. I receive
some—and I'm sure you, you'll understand—I received
some tweets, I received some, uh, Facebook messenger, all
sorts of social media attacks upon me, whether it's the private direct message that I've had to turn over to Secret Service because they are the most vile, disgusting statements
that anyone can ever receive. And when it starts to affect
your children, that's when it really affects you.

Lawrence: On January 20th, 2019, Mr. Giuliani called your
father-in-law "a criminal" and said that he may have ties to,
to organized crime. Mr. Cohen, do you believe that the
President, Mr. Giuliani, publicly targeted your father-in-law
as an effort to intimidate you? Can you elaborate? Why is
your father-in-law being pulled into this?

Cohen: I don't know the answer to that. My father-in-law was in the clothing business, um, came to this country because, in 1972-73, the expulsion of Jews from the Ukraine. He came here to this country, worked hard, and he's now enjoying his retirement. Never in my life did I think that Mr. Trump would do something so disgraceful, and he's attacking him because he knows I care about my family and to hurt me. He's trying to hurt them. Interestingly enough, my father-in-law's biggest investments happen to be in a Trump property, so it just doesn't make any sense to me.

Lawrence: I want to be clear, any efforts to prevent a witness from testifying in front of Congress is against the law. I want to be real clear about that. And as the chairman has said, retaliating against witnesses and threatening their families and members is a textbook Mob tactic that does not befit the President of the United States of this country. And I want to be on the record. This hearing is not about discrediting the President. It's about the oath of office that we take as members of Congress to have checks and balances and to meet the laws and the policies of this country we serve. Thank you, and I yield back.

Cummings: Mr. Roy.

Rep. Chip Roy (R, Texas): Mr. Cohen. Uh, I too want to offer my heartfelt thoughts for your family and what they're going through. I know it's tough and for your time here today, I know it's tough for you to stand here in front of this committee. The chairman suggested you volunteered to come here. You testified that you were asked to come here, is it correct you were asked to come here, yes or no?

Cohen: Yes.

Roy: The combined total of the crimes for which you were sentenced would bring a maximum 70 years, yes or no?

Cohen: Yes.

Roy: Yet you are going to prison for three years? Yes or no?

Cohen: Yes.

Roy: The prosecutors of the Southern District of New York say to secure loans, Cohen falsely understated the amount of debt he was carrying and omitted information from his personal financial statements to induce a bank to lend on incomplete information. You told my colleague here today that you did not commit bank fraud. Not parsing different statutes, which I understand could be, I want for clarity. Are you or are you not guilty of making false statements to a financial institution? Yes or no?

Cohen: Yes. I pled guilty.

Roy: You said clearly to Mr. Cloud and Mr. Jordan that the Southern District of New York lawyers were being untruthful in characterizing your desire to work in the administration. Do you say again that the lawyers of the Southern District of New York are being untruthful in making that characterization, yes or no?

Cohen: I'm saying that's not accurate.

Roy: Okay, so you were saying they're being untruthful—

Cohen: I'm not using the word untruthful. That's yours. I'm saying that that's not accurate. I did not want a role or title in the administration.

Roy: I'm sure the lawyers—

Cohen: I got the title that I want.

Roy: I'm sure the lawyers of the SDNY appreciate that distinction. Question you testified today, you have never been to Prague and have never been to the Czech Republic. Do you stand behind that statement?

Cohen: Yes, I do.

Roy: I offer into the record an article, uh, in known conservative news magazine, *Mother Jones* by David Corn in which he says he reviewed his notes from a phone call with Mr. Cohen that Mr. Cohen said, quote, "I haven't been to Prague in 14 years. I was in Prague for one afternoon 14 years ago." Question: You, as my friend Mr. Armstrong rightly inquired, offered to the committee taped information involving clients with a bat of an eye. Do you stand behind that? Yes or no?

Cohen: I'm sorry, I'm sorry, I don't—I don't understand you said that so fast.

Roy: You, as my friend Mr. Armstrong rightly inquired, offered to this committee, taped information involving your clients without a bat of an eye. Do you stand behind that offer?

Cohen: If the chairman asks me and it's. . .I'll take it under advisement now, and it's not a problem, in terms of attorney client privilege, yes, I will turn it over.

Roy: You, as my friend, Mr. Meadows has pointed out, misled this committee even today in a written submission that contradicted your testimony. You have suggested you are going to review that. Did you review—are you going to review it in our next break to correct the record? Yes or no?

Cohen: Yes.

Roy: Question. You helped out the President's campaign or were involved in the campaign as a representative, as a spokesman, even in your words today, it was your idea for the campaign dating back to 2011. Is that accurate? Yes or no?

Cohen: Yes.

Roy: 2011 is a year that sticks in my head, for it's the year my daughter was born, and it was the year I was diagnosed with cancer. I was not then pushing for Donald Trump to be President—I was fighting cancer. Even in 2016, I was publicly backing a certain Republican from Texas, some might guess who it was. But you, you were all in, and you either wanted Donald Trump to be your President because it would be good for the country, or you did it for your own personal advancement, or both. Sort of the two options.

Real Americans in my district and across the country wanted the President to be President, not in any way because he's perfect, but rather because they are sick and tired of this hell hole. They supported the President because they are sick and tired of the games that we are seeing here today. They are sick and tired of politicians who refuse to secure the border, balance our budget, restore health care freedom and then get the hell out of their way so they can lead their life. They're mystified that we amass about a hundred million dollars of debt per hour, which means we blown through $300, $400, $450 million during this charade in amassing debt, $450 million. They're sick and tired of a Democrat party that willfully ignores cartel driven asylum crisis on our border that endangers American citizens and the migrants who seek to come here.

Just yesterday in Eagle Pass, Texas, border patrol agents arrested an MS 13 gang member. In McAllen, Texas, federal authorities were offering a reward for a man to Mexico—tied to Mexico's Gulf cartel for his alleged roles in various murders, kidnappings, and home invasions in south Texas. And mass Honduran migrant rush at the Tex border—Texas border, force a brief closure of the Laredo port. This is this week. This is what we're ignoring. This is not what we're doing for the American people. While we engage in this charade. This is not what the American people sent us here to do. This is an embarrassment for our country.

I talked to my beautiful wife back in Dripping Springs, Texas, just before the hearing. I said, don't bother—I said, "Don't bother watching." She said, as I roughly expected, "Don't worry, I won't. I have more important things to do." And she like the rest of the American people have a hell of a lot more important things to do than to watch this. I said,

"Amen, Darling." I can't help but think that is what the majority of American people are thinking while watching this unbelievable circus. I yield back.

Cummings: Plaskett.

Rep. Stacey Plaskett (D, Virgin Islands): Thank you, Mr. Chairman. I've got a lot to do as well. Um, I've got houses and schools to help rebuild in the Virgin Islands, expansion of voting rights, educational opportunities to criminal justice reform. Thank God the Democratic majority can walk and chew gum at the same time, so we're here with you right now.

Um, Mr. Cohen, you learned well in the 10 years that you worked with Donald Trump. What was your position with the GOP in the—up to eight months ago?

Cohen: I was vice chair of the RNC finance committee.

Plaskett: You were vice chair of the finance of the Republican National Committee, right?

Cohen: Correct.

Plaskett: Okay. Um—

Cohen: I do you want to say I was a Democrat until Steve Wynn found out I was a Democrat and made me switch parties.

Plaskett: That would be a hard thing to do

Cohen: Said it wasn't right for a Democrat to be the vice chair.

Plaskett: Good. Let's get it, I don't—I only have a little bit of time. On behalf of the many members, uh, here who have expressed to your family, uh, our apologies to your family, but I want to apologize for the inappropriate comments and tweets that have been made by other members of this body. And as a former prosecutor and as former counsel on house ethics, I think that at the very least there should be a referral to the ethics committee of witness intimidation or tampering under USC 1512 of my, uh, colleague Matt Gates, and it may be possibly him being referred for criminal prosecution. So I want to put that on the record.

On May 2nd, 2018, the President's personal attorney, Rudy Giuliani, who was his personal attorney like you, appeared on Fox News and referred to the President's reimbursement to you for the 130 payment for Stephanie Clifford as part of a retainer. And on May 3rd, 2018 one day after Mr. Giuliani's appearance, the President tweeted, and I quote, "Mr. Cohen and attorney received a monthly retainer not from the campaign and having nothing to do with the campaign from which he entered into through an imbursement, a private contract, between two parties known as a nondisclosure agreement or NDA."

The office of government ethics, which is the agency which the federal government, with responsibility over what the President needs to report publicly about his assets, was puzzled by this, it seems. And they were skeptical that a retainer was actually in place, and asked to see the retainer agreement on call, uh, of May 8th with the President. The President's personal counsel, Sheri Dillon, replied that she would, and I quote, "Not permit OGE staff to read the agreement because it is privilege. Ms. Dylan would not even let OGE staff to come to her office to review the retainer agreement. Mr. Cohen, in a court filing August of last year, federal prosecutors stated that quote, "In truth and in fact, there was no such retainer agreement." Mr. Cohen, did you ever have a retainer agreement in place with the President for the payment to Ms. Clifford?

Cohen: No.

Plaskett: So was Mr. Giuliani's statement inaccurate?

Cohen: Yes.

Plaskett: Was Ms. Dylan's statement about the retainer agreement inaccurate?

Cohen: I'm sorry, Dylan's statement is?

Plaskett: About the retainer agreement. Is it inaccurate?

Cohen: And her statement, her statement is what?

Plaskett: And her statement to them was quote, uh, "Not to permit OGE staff to read the agreement because it is privilege."

Cohen: There was no agreement.

Plaskett: And is the President's tweet or his statement accurate.

Cohen: And I'm sorry, one more time?

Plaskett: And his statement was, Mr. Cohen, "An attorney received a monthly retainer not from the campaign and having nothing to do with the campaign from which he entered in through, through a reimbursement."

Cohen: That's not accurate.

Plaskett: Um, you've mentioned some individuals to my colleague from New York, Ms. Connolly, and also in your testimony, about Mr. Weisselberg and other individuals, Ms. Rhona. Who are those individuals? Uh, are they with the Trump organization?

Cohen: There are.

Plaskett: Are there other people that we should be meeting with?

Cohen: Allen Weisselberg is the chief financial officer.

Plaskett: You got to quickly give us as many names as you can so we can get to them.

Cohen: Yes ma'am.

Plaskett: Ms. Rhona's—what is Ms. Rhona's position?

Cohen: Rhona Graff is the—Mr. Trump's executive assistant.

Plaskett: And would she be able to corroborate many of the statements that you've made here?

Cohen: Yes, she was—her office is directly next to his, and she's involved in a lot that went on.

Plaskett: Okay. Mr. Cohen, when the President's lawyers were having the discussions with the Office of Government Ethics in 2018, did they reach out to you to talk with you about these payments?

Cohen: No ma'am.

Plaskett: And what did you, did you share anything with them otherwise in any other conversation?

Cohen: I do not recall, no.

Plaskett: Can the committee obtain more information about these facts by obtaining testimony documents from the White House, the Trump organization, and the President's attorneys?

Cohen: I believe so.

Plaskett: Uh, Mr. Chair, I think that those are the individuals that we should be speaking with. Um, and I yield back at this time.

Cummings: Committee will now stand in recess again. We will come back—listen up 30, 35 minutes, 35 minutes after the last vote begins. So for Mr. Cohen, Mr. Cohen, we're talking about probably about an hour, about an hour or so.

Cohen: Thank you so much.

RECESS

Cummings: Ladies and gentlemen, we will come to order. Mr. Cohen, I want to finalize this issue relating to your truth in testimony form. Uh, the form requires you to list your contracts or payments originating from a foreign government, a nod from all foreign entities who we said we would give you a chance to consult with your attorneys. Have you done that in, do you have any additional information?

Cohen: My four attorneys continue to believe as they did before, that the language of the truth and testimony form which I was given and signed it just right before this hearing and which requires disclosure, of any contracts or payments from foreign governments in the last two years did not apply to my work for BTA Bank, which has Kazakh-owned entity. They advise that had entities been intended for disclosure, that word would have been in the disclosure definition. However, if the committee's counsel has a different view that I should disclose my contract with BTA bank, we'd be willing to do that.

Meadows: Mr. Chairman?

Cummings: Um, let me finish. Sure. Um, I want to understand clearly you are, you sought the advice of your counsel, is that right?

Cohen: That's correct.

Cummings: And your counsel or advise you to say what you just said, is that right?

Cohen: That's correct.

Cummings: And you know that to be the truth. Is that right?

Cohen: Yes sir.

Cummings: I will yield to the gentleman from . . .

Meadows: I thank the Chairman for his courtesy. Mr. Chairman, instead of making points of order and going back and forth on this, perhaps a way to solve this is for the chairman to request Mr. Cohen give to this committee all the foreign payments that he has received over the last two years, whether they're an entity or a government, because we have strong belief, Mr. Chairman, there's over $900,000 that came from the government of Kazakhstan on behalf of Mr. Cohen. And, and it is either the truth, the whole truth and nothing but the truth and, and the rules. Mr. Chairman, uh, really look at foreign payments that come from or with foreign governments and, and the bank he's talking about is owned 81% by the Kazakhstan government.

Cummings: Reclaiming my time, reclaiming my time. And then we're going to move on. What I will take, I will, first of all, let me be clear, I said to Mr. Cohen, uh, that if he came in here and lied, I would nail him to the cross. Didn't I?

Cohen: Yes, he did. More than once.

Cummings: All right. Um, so if there's any ambiguity, I want that to be clear that I have no problem in working with you to make sure that straightened out because I don't, I don't want it to be a thing where he thinks one thing, we think one thing, and we can, we can clear that up. All right? We have a number of members that we've been waiting.

Jordan: Just on that subject, I said, Mr. Chairman, I don't think we should be limited just to the BTA bank, which has the affiliation with Kazakhstan. I think we should also look at Korea Aerospace Industries, one of his other clients, and any other client that's foreign that may have some connection to that respective country's government. I hope him and his attorneys look at all those and we get the phone exactly right as Mr. Meadows wants.

Cummings: Reclaiming my time. Uh, we will take that certainly under advisement. You are, I'm a man of my word. We will do, we will work with you and see what we can, uh, to come up with that. I don't think that it's an unreasonable request. Mr. Khanna. Hello?

Rep. Ro Khanna (D, California): Mr. Cohen, I want to focus my questions on the smoking gun document you have provided this committee. This document is compelling evidence of federal and state crimes including financial fraud. You provided this committee with a check from President Donald J. Trump's revocable trust account, which is marked as Exhibit 5B. It is a check for $35,000 and it is dated March 17, 2017, after the President took office. It's right now on the screen. Do you see it, sir?

Cohen: Yes, sir.

Khanna: To be clear, the Trump revocable trust is the trust the President set up to hold his assets after he became President. Is that correct?

Cohen: I believe so.

Khanna: Do you know why you were paid from the trust as opposed to the President's personal account?

Cohen: I don't know the answer to that.

Khanna: Did you think it was odd that he paid you once from his personal account and then he's paying you through the scheme of a trust?

Cohen: I'll be honest, I was just happy to get the check today.

Khanna: You testified that the check was signed by Donald Trump Jr. and the Trump Organization CFO Allen Weisselberg, is that correct?

Cohen: That is correct.

Khanna: According to the criminal charges against you, you sent monthly invoices containing false information to an individual identified as Executive 1. Weisselberg is Executive 1, correct?

Cohen: Yes.

Khanna: The criminal charge against you then states that Executive 1 forwarded your invoice to someone referred to as Executive 2—presumably Donald Trump, Jr., who was signing this check as Executive 2. Correct?

Cohen: I believe so.

Khanna: As federal prosecutors laid out in their criminal charges, payments like this check resulted in numerous false statements in the books and records of the Trump Organization, and it's important for the American public to understand it has nothing to do with collusion. This is financial fraud, garden variety, financial fraud. It was disguised as a payment for legal services to you, but this was not a payment for legal services, was it, Mr. Cohen?

Cohen: No, sir.

Khanna: It could give rise to serious state and federal criminal liability if a corporation is cooking its books. Based on your testimony today, Donald Trump Jr. and Allen Weisselberg directed this payment to you and approved this payment. Is that right?

Cohen: Mr. Trump initially acknowledged the obligation, the debt. Myself and Allen Weisselberg went back to his office, and I was instructed by Allen at the time that they were going to do this over 12 installments. And what he decided to do then was to have me send an invoice, in which case they can have a check cut and then, yes, the answer would be yes to your two-year follow-up.

Khanna: And Donald Trump Jr. obviously signed off on this.

Cohen: Yes, it was. It would either be Eric Trump, Donald Trump Jr., and/or Allen Weisselberg, but always Allen Weisselberg on the check.

Khanna: And you think Executive 2 is Donald Trump Jr.

Cohen: Yes.

Khanna: They knew that this payment, uh, was false and illegal, correct?

Cohen: I, I can make that conclusion.

Khanna: You told representative Kelly that the President was aware of this scheme, is that correct?

Cohen: That's correct.

Khanna: I just want the American public to understand that the explosive nature of your current testimony in this document. Are you telling us, Mister Cohen, that the President directed transactions in conspiracy with Allen Weisselberg and his son Donald Trump Jr. as part of a civil criminal, as part of a criminal conspiracy of financial fraud? Is that your testimony today?

Cohen: Yes.

Khanna: And do you know if this criminal financial scheme that the President, Allen Weisselberg, and Donald Trump Jr. are involved in is being investigated by the Southern District in New York?

Cohen: I'd rather not discuss that question because it could be part of an investigation that's currently ongoing,

Khanna: But I just want the American public to understand that it's wholly apart from Bob Mueller's investigation. There is garden variety financial fraud, and your allegation and the explosive smoking gun documents suggest that the President, his son, and his CFO may be involved in a criminal conspiracy. And isn't it true, Mr. Cohen, that this criminal conspiracy that involved four people, that there's only one person so far who's suffered the repercussions, and that's why you're in jail.

Cohen: Will be going to jail, yes.

Khanna: There are three other people, though, who were equally involved in this conspiracy.

Cohen: Yeah, that's true. It is true.

Khanna: Thank you, Mr. Cohen. I yield back my time.

Cummings: Gomez.

Rep. Jimmy Gomez (D, California): Thank you, Mr. Chair. Mr. Cohen, I'm going to tackle the President's tax returns during the 2016 campaign. You said you personally wouldn't, quote, "allow him to release those returns until the audits are over," unquote. Uh, for the record, nothing prevents individuals from sharing their own tax returns, even while under audit by the IRS. Mr. Cohen, do you know whether President Trump's tax returns were really under audit by the IRS in 2016?

Cohen: I don't know the answer. I asked for a copy of the audit so that I could use it in terms of my, um, statements to the press, and I was never able to obtain one.

Gomez: Okay. So do you have any inside knowledge about what was in the President's tax returns that he refused to release?

Cohen: I do not.

Gomez: Can you give us any insight into what the real reason is that the President has refused to release his tax returns?

Cohen: The statements that he had said to me was that what he didn't want was to have an entire group of think tanks that are tax experts run through his tax return and start ripping it to pieces, and then he'll end up in an audit and ultimately have, um, taxable consequences, penalties, and so on.

Gomez: So that's an interesting point that basically he said he didn't want to release his tax returns because he might end up in an audit. So could you presume from that statement that he wasn't under audit?

Cohen: I presume that he's not under audit.

Gomez: And the reason why I bring this up, cause I'm also the only Democrat on this committee that also serves on the Committee of Ways and Means—it's the chief tax writing committee in the House of Representatives, and it's the only committee in the House of Representatives that has jurisdiction to request an American's tax returns. And that includes the President of the United States. My constituents need to know whether the President has financial ties that are causing him to protect his own bottom line rather than the best interest of this country. Can he be blackmailed because of his financial and business ventures, including by foreign governments? And I know the top position is the first thing they're going to ask or say is that he released as a financial disclosure forms. But I believe that there's other things we can learn from his taxes. Do you know, do you have any idea what we can learn in his tax returns if we actually received, we got our hands on them?

Cohen: No, I've actually, I've seen them. I just have never gone through them. They're quite long, quite long.

Gomez: Um, one of the things I also find ironic is that the way they're kind of attacking you as to undermine your credibility is, one of the ways is by saying that you committed bank fraud and tax evasion. And the reason why it's a big deal is that it really goes down to the people, a person's character, when it comes to taxes. But yet the, the Republican minority has never asked to see his taxes. Right? Something that for 40 years, Democrats and Republicans alike have released their tax returns to prove to the American people that they didn't have financial interests that would be leverageable by a foreign government. But this minority refuses to ask for his tax returns. Um, I also want to kind of, um, I'm noticing a pattern. I'm noticing a pattern about the President and those in his inner circle. Special Counsel, Robert Mueller's team has indicted or receive guilty pleas from 34 people and three companies that we know of—the latest, big long-term Trump advisor Roger Stone. That group includes six former Trump advisors. It appears that the President has a fondness for entrusting those who will (1) lie for him, (2) break the law for him, (3) cheat the system for him. Essentially he wants to surround himself with people who are just like him. Would you agree with that statement?

Cohen: From the facts and circumstances, it appears so.

Gomez: So Mr. Cohen, the American people have a lot of questions when it comes to this President, to his conduct, when he went to Helsinki and he bowed before, uh, Vladimir Putin. And nobody can really understand why he acts the way he acts. And we believe that the way we get those answers is really looking at everybody that surrounds him, who he's been associated with, and his tax returns because that is the only way that we can get down to the, to the bottom line. Thank you. And I yield back.

Meadows: Mr. Chairman, Mr. Chairman, and I have a unanimous consent request.

Cummings: All right, go ahead.

Meadows: Um, I ask unanimous consent that we read into, for the record, a tweet from Dr. Darrell Scott, which says, "Michael Cohen asked—no, begged me, repeatedly—to ask POTUS to give him a job in the administration. He is still lying under oath." I ask unanimous consent.

Cummings: No objections.

Meadows: I have one more, uh, from Bob Deedle, uh, "Getting sick watching these hearings. I've known Michael Cohen personally for many years and he told me several times that he was very angry and upset that he didn't get a post in the White House and that he would do any, do what he has to do now to protect his family." Close quote. I asked that that be . . .

Cummings: No objections.

Meadows: I thank you.

Jordan: Mr. Chairman, two quick ones.

Cummings: If you've got other ones, what are we going to do you, Mr. Ranking Member, and then we'll do the other ones at the end because I have some things to the I want to get in.

Jordan: I asked unanimous consent that an article in Salon magazine written by Stanley Brand, former house counsel to Tip O'Neill. The title of the article is "Oversight Committee Session with Michael Cohen Looks Like an Illegitimate Show Hearing." I ask unanimous consent that a letter that Mr. Meadows and I sent to you, the Chairman, uh, requesting that you call Deputy Attorney General Rod Rosenstein to testify at this hearing also be part of the record. Thank you.

Cohen: Mr. Chairman, can I respond?

Cummings: Just one second. All right. Um, the article by Mr. Brand, I just want to deal with this and right away, um, we, when we saw that article, um, Mr. Ranking Member, uh, we knew that it was inaccurate. I mean, just on basics. I mean the case is that Mr. Brand's views are definitely distinguishable for what's going on here. And so we got, uh, Irvin B. Nathan, former general counsel of the House from 2007 to 2010, and she says, in short, the court has ample jurisdiction and responsibility to hear and consider the upcoming voluntary testimony and Michael Cohen. That's dated February 25, 2019. And uh, I want to enter that into record without objection. So ordered. Um, where are we? Ocasio-Cortez.

Rep. Alexandria Ocasio-Cortez (D, New York): Thank you, Mr. Chair. Mr. Cohen, I'd like to quickly pick up on some previous lines of questioning before getting into my own, so I may go a little quickly to get it all in five minutes. Uh, first my colleague from Vermont had asked you, asked several questions about AMI, the parent company of the *National Enquirer.* And uh, in that you mentioned a treasure trove, quote, "treasure trove" of documents in David Pecker's office relating to information assembled from all these catch-and-kill operations against people who potentially had damaging information on the President. You also mentioned that the President was very concerned about the whereabouts of these documents and who possessed them. Does that treasure trove of documents still exist?

Cohen: I don't know. I had asked David Pecker for them. So you would say the person who knows the whereabouts of these documents would be David Pecker, Barry Levine or, um, Dylan Howard.

Ocasio-Cortez: Okay, thank you. Um, secondly, I want to ask a little bit about your conversation with my colleague from Missouri about asset inflation. To your knowledge, did the President ever provide inflated assets to an insurance company?

Cohen: Yes.

Ocasio-Cortez: Who else knows that the President did this?

Cohen: Allen Weisselberg, Ron Leiberman, and Matthew Calamari.

Ocasio-Cortez: And where would the committee find more information on this? Do you think we need to review his financial statements and his tax returns in order to compare them?

Cohen: Yes. And you'd find it at the Trump Org.

Ocasio-Cortez: Thank you very much. Uh, the last, last thing here, the Trump golf organization currently has a golf course in my home borough of the Bronx: Trump Links. I drive past it every day, going between the Bronx and Queens. Um, in fact, the *Washington Post* reported on the Trump Links Bronx course in an article entitled "Taxpayers Built This New York Golf Course, and Trump Reaps the Rewards." That article is where many New Yorkers and people in the country learned that taxpayers spent $127 million to build Trump Links in a, quote, "generous deal allowing President Trump to keep almost every dollar that flows in on a golf course built with public funds."

And it doesn't seem to be the only time the President has benefited at the expense of the public. Mr. Cohen, I want to ask you about your assertion that the President may have improperly devalued his assets to avoid paying taxes. According to an August 24—August 21, 2016 report by the *Washington Post*, while the President claimed in financial disclosure forms that Trump national golf club in Jupiter, Florida was worth more than $50 million, he had reported otherwise to local tax authorities that the course was worth quote "no more than $5 million." Mr. Cohen, do you know whether this specific report is accurate?

Cohen: It's identical to what he did at Trump national golf club at Briar Cliff Manor.

Ocasio-Cortez: Do you know, to your knowledge, was the President interested in reducing his local real estate bills tax bills?

Cohen: Yes.

Ocasio-Cortez: And how did he do that?

Cohen: What you do is you deflate the value of the asset and then you put in a request to the tax department for a deduction.

Ocasio-Cortez: Thank you. Now, in October 2018 the *New York Times* revealed that quote, "President Trump participated in dubious tax schemes during the 1990s including instances of outright fraud that greatly increased the fortune he received from his parents." It further stated for Mr. Trump, quote, "He also helped formulate a strategy to undervalue his parents real estate holdings by hundreds of millions of dollars on tax returns, sharply reducing his tax bill when those properties were transferred to him and his siblings." Mr. Cohen, do you know whether that specific report is accurate?

Cohen: I don't. I wasn't there in 1990s.

Ocasio-Cortez: Who would know the answer to those questions?

Cohen: Allen Weisselberg.

Ocasio-Cortez: And would it help for the committee to obtain federal and state tax returns from the President and his company to address that discrepancy?

Cohen: I believe so.

Ocasio-Cortez: Thank you very much. I yield the rest of my time to the chair.

Cummings: Ms. Pressley.

Rep. Ayanna Pressley (D, Massachusetts): Thank you, Mr. Chairman. Um, one more time, Mr. Chairman, I just want to thank you for your leadership and the way in which you comport yourself. And I know there was some that would have you believe that the more you say something, the more true it is, but in fact this committee, thanks to your leadership and our democratic majority, has been joined the work of the American people. Before this committee alone we looked at the issue of making election day a federal holiday, reducing drug pricing, uh, and pursued subpoenas to reunite families. And just recently, uh, before we returned here, tried to pass a universal background check gun bill. So we're doing the business of the American people, including today.

It has been said that the sunlight is said to be the best of disinfectants. Electric light is the most efficient policemen. Well let there be light because the point of oversight is for us to pursue the trust, to pursue the truth and justice of the American people, to understand if lies, deceit, and corruption are threatening American democracy and, indeed, our safety. Mr. Chairman, charities should not be abused as personal piggy banks. It is both against the law and extremely unfair to charities that play by the rules. A line of questioning that we have not yet addressed and we've been glaringly absent in tackling is that of the abuses of the

Trump Foundation. Now, the President's charitable foundation agreed to dissolve in response to an ongoing investigation and lawsuit by the New York Attorney General. The New York Attorney General found what it called, quote, "clear and repeated violations of state and federal law," including, quote, "repeated and a willful self-dealing by the Trump administration"—apologies, "by the foundation." If I understand your opening statement correctly, in mid 2013 you arranged for a straw purchaser to pay $60,000 for a portrait of Mr. Trump painted by the artist William Quigley at a charity auction. Is that correct?

Cohen: That's correct.

Pressley: Why would the President want to bid up the price of something he was ultimately paying for?

Cohen: It was all about ego.

Pressley: How was it paid for?

Cohen: I believe it was paid for by check from the trust?

Pressley: An abuse, and again, you know, uh, this is not a partisan pursuit here. I think what ultimately we're demonstrating is patriotism. This is about what is right and just for the American people. Did the straw purchaser purchase the painting and then the foundation funds reimbursed the straw purchaser? Can you explain the mechanics of that payment?

Cohen: Well, I'm, I'm not involved with the foundation.

Pressley: Okay. Did the President know what was happening?

Cohen: Oh yes.

Pressley: And how did you know who knew what was happening?

Cohen: Because he tasked me to find the straw bidder to ensure that his painting, which was going last in the auction, would go for the highest amount of any of the paintings that have been put on the auction block for the day.

Pressley: And what happened to the painting?

Cohen: I believe it's in one of the clubs.

Pressley: Okay. Um, according to the New York attorney general, in March 2014 Mr. Trump again used the foundation to pay $10,000 for the winning bid on another portrait of Mr. Trump that ended up as decor in one of his golf courses in Miami. Mr. Cohen, are you familiar with that transaction?

Cohen: Yes.

Pressley: Are you aware of any other instances where the Trump Foundation was used to benefit the Trump family?

Cohen: Yes.

Pressley: Could you elaborate?

Cohen: So there was a contract that I ended up, um, creating on Mr. Trump's behalf for a Ukrainian oligarch by the name of Victor Pinchuk, and it was that Mr. Trump was asked to coming to participate in what was the Ukrainian American Economic Forum. Unfortunately, he wasn't able to go, but I was able to negotiate 15 minutes by Skype where they would have a camera, very much like a television camera, very much like that one. And they would translate Mr. Trump to the questioner, and then he would respond back, and I negotiated a fee of $150,000 for 15 minutes. I was directed by Mr. Trump to have the contract done in the name of the Donald J. Trump Foundation as opposed to Donald J. Trump for services rendered.

Pressley: Thank you. Any other abuses of the foundation that you'd like to share? Again, it is against the law, and, again, extremely unfair to charities that are playing by the rules.

Cohen: Not at this time, but if I think of one . . .

Pressley: Okay, excellent. And then for the balance of my time, would you agree that uh, someone could deny rental units to African Americans, lead the birther movement, referred to the Diaspora as "shithole countries," and refer to white supremacists as "fine people," have a black friend, and still be racist?

Cohen: Yes.

Pressley: I agree.

Cummings: The young lady's time has expired. You may answer the question.

Cohen: I did. Yes.

Meadows: Mr. Chairman, I have two unanimous consent since we're, we're finishing up. Before we get done, I want to go ahead and . . .

Cummings: Okay, just gimme gimme gimme one second. I just want . . . Yes, sir. I wanted to get to Ms. Tlaib and I'll come to you. Okay. Ms. Tlaib and then they've been waiting all day. Ms. Tlaib?

Rep. Rashida Tlaib (D, Michigan): Thank you, Mr. Chairman. Thank you. All of you. First centering this committee on our sole purpose, um, is exposing the truth, and some of my colleagues can't handle the truth, and this is unfortunate because it's the center of what is protecting our country right now. The people at home are frustrated, and Mr. Cohen and they want criminal schemes to stop, especially those from the Oval Office. Mr. Cohen, I am upset and know that my residents feel the same way that the man you worked for the past 10 years is using the most powerful position in the world to hurt our country solely for personal gain. We are upset that some of our colleagues here are so disconnected from what means what it means to have this President of the United States sending checks to cover bribe payments—not hush payments, bribe payments—you made on his behalf, one in 2000 and 17th of March and another in August 2017 after he was sworn in as President. They are upset that while my colleagues are trying to discredit your testimony by some of your own unlawful acts and lies that they are disconnected with the fact that you were the personal lawyer for this President of the United States, that this President chose you as his legal counsel.

My stance has always been the same. Mr. Chairman, based on the facts, not on future reports that we're all waiting on, my residents back home don't need a collusion case with a foreign government to know this President, Individual 1, has disregarded the law of the land, the United States Constitution, and that he has misused his powers. In the sentencing memo, Mr. Cohen, filed by the federal prosecutors in New York in December of last year, they stated, quote, "In particular and as Cohen himself has now admitted with respect to both payments, he acted in coordination with and at the direction of Individual 1." Mr. Cohen, as you know, President Donald J. Trump brand comes first, not the American people. Based on what you know now, based on what we know now, is that individual one used his money, businesses, and platform to enrich himself, his brand, and then in the process directed you, Mr. Cohen, to commit multiple fennel—felonies—and you covered it up, correct?

Cohen: That's correct.

Tlaib: You called it protecting his brand?

Cohen: Correct. And him as well.

Tlaib: Mr. Cohen, with this, do you think the President of the United States is making decisions in the best interest of the American people?

Cohen: No, I don't.

Tlaib: Especially those you said that he used horrible words about, like African Americans, Muslim Americans, and immigrants?

Cohen: Yes.

Tlaib: Just to make a note, Mr. Chairman, just because someone has a person of color, a black person working for them does not mean they aren't racist, and it is insensitive that some would even say, the fact that someone would actually use a prop, a black woman in this chamber, in this committee, is alone racist in itself. Donald Trump is setting a precedent . . .

Meadows: Mr. Chairman I ask that her words be taken down.

Tlaib: Donald Trump is setting a precedent—I am reclaiming my time—Donald Trump is setting a precedent . . .

Meadows: Mr. Chairman. Mr. Chairman.

Tlaib: . . . that the highest office can be attained . . .

Meadows: Mr. Chairman, the rules are clear.

Tlaib: . . . actually cover up and hold onto business assets to break campaign finance law and constitutional clauses. What we have here, Mr. Chairman, it's criminal conduct, and the pursuit of the highest public office by Mr. Cohen and Individual 1. I hope that the gravity of this situation hits everyone in this body, the court report, and in Congress and across this country. Thank you, Mr. Chairman. I yield the rest of my time.

Meadows: Mr. Chairman, I asked that her words when she's referring to an individual member of this body be taken down and stricken from the record. I am sure she didn't intend to do this, but if anyone knows my record as it relates, it should be you, Mr. Chairman.

Jordan: Chairman, I would like to hold on. I want the words right back.

Cummings: Hold on. No, no, no, no.

Jordan: We want to know exactly what she said about a colleague.

Cummings: Excuse me. Would you like to rephrase that statement, Ms. Tlaib?

Tlaib: Thank you, Mr. Chairman. I can actually read it from here: Just to make a note, Mr. Chairman, that just because someone has a person of color, a black person working for them does not mean they aren't racist. And it is insensitive that someone would even say it as racist in itself and to use a black woman as a prop to move to prove it otherwise. And I can submit this for the record if a colleague is thinking that that's what I'm saying, I'm just saying that's what I believe to have happened. And if as a person of color in this committee, that's how I felt at that moment and I wanted to express that, but I am not calling the gentlemen, um, Mr. Meadows, a racist for doing so. I'm saying that in itself it is a racist act.

Meadows: Well I hope not, Mr. Chairman, because I need to be clear on this. Mr. Chairman . . .

Cummings: Mister Meadow. Wait a minute,

Meadows: I've defended you and . . .

Cummings: Mr. Meadows! I'm the chair. Thank you. All right. I will clear this up. Now Ms. Tlaib, I want to make sure I understand. You did not, you were not intending to call Mr. Meadows a racist, is that right?

Tlaib: No, Mr. Meadows, I do not call Mr. Meadows a racist. I am trying, as a person of color, Mr. Chairman, just to express myself and how I felt at that moment and so just for the record, that's what was my intention.

Cummings: Yeah. Better. That's better.

Meadows: Mr. Chairman, there's nothing more personal to me than my relationship. My nieces and nephew are people of color. Not many people know that. You know that Mr. Chairman, and to indicate that I asked someone who is a personal friend of the, the Trump family who has worked for him, who knows this particular individual, that she's coming in to be a prop. It's racist to suggest that I ask her to come in here for that reason. Mr. President, the President's own person, she's a family member and she, she loves these, this family she came in because she felt like the President of the United States was getting falsely accused. Him and Mr. Chairman, you are, you and I have a personal relationship. It's not based on color and, and to even go down this direction is wrong, Mr. Chairman.

Cummings: First of all, I want to thank you gentlemen for what you have stated. Um, if there's anyone who is sensitive to with regard to race is me, son of former sharecroppers that were basically slaves. So I get it. Yeah. Um, I listened very carefully to Ms. Tlaib, and I think, and I don't want to put, I'm not going to put words in her mouth, but I think she said that she was not calling you a racist. And I thought that we could clarify that because you, Mr. Meadows, you know, uh, and of all the people on this committee—I've said it and got in trouble for it—that you're one of my best friends. I know that shocks a lot of people.

Meadows: Likewise, Mr. Chairman.

Cummings: But you are, and I would do and I could see and feel your pain. I feel it. And so, and I don't think Ms. Tlaib intended to cause you that, that kind of pain and that kind of frustration. Did you have a statement, Ms. Tlaib, and we can just straighten this up.

Tlaib: And, and to my colleague, Mr. Meadows, that was not my intention. And I do apologize if that's what it sounded like, but I said "someone" in general, and as everybody knows in this chamber, I'm pretty direct. So, if I wanted to say that I would have, but that's not what I said. And, uh, thank you, Mr. Chairman, for allowing me to clar-

ify it. But again, I said "someone," and again, was not referring to you at all as a racist.

Meadows: Well, I, I thank the gentlewoman for her comments, I thank the Chairman for, uh, working to clarify
this. And, um, and I, I appreciate the, the chairman's, uh,
intervening.

Cummings: No, no, thanks to the gentleman. Um, first of
all, thank you for allowing us to resolve that. Um, the gentleman had asked a little bit earlier. . .

Meadows: I will withdraw my request.

Cummings: Oh, you don't want to do the, uh, the anony-
mous consent?

Meadows: I'm saying I need the unanimous consent . . . I
think I need to officially withdraw my request and it will be
stricken.

Cummings: Um, now I will recognize you for your unanimous consent. I think you want to put in the records
documents.

Meadows: Yeah. Thank you, Mr. Chairman. I ask you unanimous consent that we, uh, put forth in the record the *Vanity Fair* article, which indicates that Michael Cohen must be
the most gifted consultant in the, in America, uh, outlining
his insights into government healthcare and policy and real
estate, suggesting that he's not, it's not a real company, but
uh, and just like he's not a lawyer without objection.

Cummings: So ordered.

Meadows: Thank you. I ask unanimous consent that the *LA Times* article of July 16, 2018, uh, actually be put in the record, which outlines the $1.2 million payment and their misgivings thereafter without objection.

Cummings: So ordered. Any other, uh, unanimous consent request? Hice.

Hice: Thank you, Mr. Chairman. Uh, I ask unanimous consent to make the February 9, 2019 *Washington Post* profile of Michael Cohen titled "Michael Cohen's Secret Agenda" part of the record. This story shows Cohen to be a selfish manipulator who is all about himself. It even has a false anecdote about how he once claimed at deliver his own son, his own baby.

Cummings: Without objection. So ordered.

Hice: Thank you, Mr. Chairman. I ask unanimous consent to make the May 9, 2018 *Washington Post* article "South Korean Firm Paid Michael Cohen $150,000 as It Sought Contract from U.S. Government" as part of the record. The article reported Korea Aerospace Industries paid a shell company run by Cohen.

Cummings: Without objection. So ordered.

Hice: Thank you, Mr. Chairman. I ask unanimous consent to make Michael Cohen's sentencing statement to the Southern District of New York part of the record. A statement establishes that Michael Cohen continues to falsely blame his crimes on blind loyalty to the President, but only Cohen is to blame for his many false statements to financial institutions and the IRS.

Cummings: Without objection. So ordered.

Hice: I'm asking unanimous consent to make the August 20, 2018 CNN article: "Feds Scrutinizing Michael Cohen's Former Accountant and Bank Loans" part of the record. Cohen's accountant was subpoenaed to appear before grand jury and required a lawyer. In his sentencing memo prosecutors said Cohen attempted to blame his tax evasion on his accountant.

Cummings: Without objection. So ordered.

Hice: Two more. Real quickly. Sure. Ask unanimous consent to make the February 26, 2019 order filed by the appellate division of the State of New York regarding disciplinary proceedings against Michael Cohen part of the record. This order, which proactively applies starting February 28th establishes Cohen committed a serious crime and ceased being an attorney when he was convicted of lying to Congress.

Cummings: Without objection. So ordered.

Hice: And finally, Mr. Chairman, I ask you unanimous consent to make the July 26, 2018 *Washington Post* article "Michael Cohen Secretly Recorded Trump. Does That Make Him a Bad Lawyer?" part of the record. The article describes potential ethical violations of a lawyer Cohen recording his client Trump without the client's knowledge.

Cummings: Without objection. So ordered. Mr. Norman.

Norman: Thank you, Mr. Chairman. I ask unanimous consent to make the January 18, 2019 *Huffington Post* article "11 Tweets from the Fake Fan Account 'Stud' Michael Cohen Paid to Fawn Over Him" part of the record. The account is described as a place for "women who love and support Michael Cohen. Strong, pit bull, sex symbol, no nonsense, business oriented, and ready to make waves."

Cummings: Without objection. So ordered. Mr. Roy.

Roy: Thank you, Mr. Chairman. Uh, I would ask unanimous consent to make the April 20, 2018 article in *Mother Jones* titled "Michael Cohen Says He's Never Been to Prague. He Told Me a Different Story" a part of the record.

Cummings: Without objection, so ordered.

Roy: Thank you, sir.

Cummings: Got it. Very well. I have some concluding remarks, but before I do that, um, do you have anything you'd like to say?

Cohen: Yes, yes, Mr. Chairman, I would, I have some closing remarks. I would like to save myself. Is this an appropriate . . .

Cummings: You can do it now.

Cohen: Thank you. So first I want to thank you, Chairman, because I appreciate the opportunity to share some final thoughts. I've acknowledged I have made my own mistakes and I have owned up to them publicly and under oath, but silence and complicity in the face of the daily destruction of our basic norms and civility to one another will not be one of them. I did things and I acted improperly at times and Mr. Trump's behest, I blindly followed his demands. My loyalty to Mr. Trump has cost me everything: my family's happiness, friendships, my law license, my company, my livelihood, my honor, my reputation, and soon my freedom, and I will not sit back, say nothing, and allow him to do the same to the country. Indeed, given my experience working for Mr. Trump, I fear that if he loses the election in 2020 that there will never be a peaceful transition of power. And this is why I agreed to appear before you today.

In closing, I would like to say directly to the President, we honor our veterans, even in the rain. You tell the truth, even when it doesn't aggrandize you. You respect the law and our incredible law enforcement agents and don't villainize them. You don't disparage generals, Gold Star families, prisoners of war, and other heroes who had the courage to fight for this country. You don't attack the media and those who question what you don't like or what you don't want them to say. And you take responsibility for your own dirty deeds. You don't use your power of your bully pulpit to destroy the credibility of those who speak out against you. You don't separate families from one another or demonize those looking to America for a better life. You don't vilify people based on the God they pray to and you don't cuddle up to our adversaries at the expense of our allies. And finally, you don't shut down the government before Christmas and New Years just to simply appease your base. This behavior is churlish. It denigrates the office of the President and it's simply un-American. And it's not you.

So, to those who support the President and his rhetoric, as I once did, I pray the country doesn't make the same mistakes that I have made or paid the heavy price that my family and I are paying. And I thank you very much for this additional time, Chairman. Thank you very much.

Cummings: The ranking member has closing statement.

Jordan: Thank you, Mr. Chairman. Uh, we know Mr. Cohen has been dishonest in the past. That's why he's going to prison in two months. But there are things today that he said during the several hours of questioning that just don't add up either. He said he never defrauded any bank when he was having a conversation questioning from Mr. Comer. Obviously that's not true because he's going to prison for that very offense. He said today he was a good lawyer who understood the need to represent his client, his client with legal advice. But in his written testimony, he said he never bothered to consider whether payments to women for improper, much less the right thing to do. He attested in his signed truth and testimony form that he'd not had any reportable contracts with foreign government entities. Earlier, he admitted to having consulting agreements with that lists at least two foreign entities owned in part by foreign governments: BTA Bank of Kazakhstan and Korean Aerospace Industries of South Korea. He said to Chairman Cummings that Donald Trump directed him and the

Trump Organization, CFO, Allen Weisselberg, to quote, "go back to his office and figure out how to make $130,000 payment." But in his testimony, he says Mr. Trump "directed me to use my own personal funds from the home equity line of credit to avoid any money being traced back to him that could negatively impact the campaign." And in response to a question about him paying to set up the fake Twitter account @WomenForCohen, that he didn't direct the commission of that Twitter account. He says, "I didn't set that up. And it was done by a young lady that works with the firm" when, in fact, he did ask the IT firm Redfinch to set it up, according to the owner of Redfinch. And finally, he said he didn't want a job with the administration, even though the attorneys with the Southern District of New York stated that this was a fact. When asked about this, Cohen said, "I wouldn't call them liars, but that statement is not accurate."

Mr. Chairman, I think maybe more importantly is what we should have been doing today. Mr. Meadow and I sent you a letter asking you to have Mr. Rosenstein here. I think it's important to know that last week when you announced that Mr. Cohen was coming this week just happened to be the very same week that we learned the Deputy Attorney General of the United States was thinking about wearing a wire to record the Commander-In-Chief, was actually contemplating talking to Cabinet members and invoking the 25th amendment. That's what we should be focused on— not this sad display we've had to go through the last several hours. And again, it's not my words. You can take the words of the former general counsel for the House of Representatives under tip O'Neill. So, I hope we've learned some things here today. Um, but Mr. Chairman, as I said earlier, your first big hearing, the first announced witness of the 116th Congress is a gentleman who is going to prison in two months for lying to Congress. I don't think that's what we should be focused on. I yield back.

Cummings: Thank you very much. You know I've sat here, and I've listened to all this, and it's very painful. It's very painful. You made a lot of mistakes, Mr. Cohen—and you've admitted that. And, you know, one of the saddest parts of this whole thing is that some very innocent people are hurting too. And you acknowledged that. And, um, that's your family.

And, so you come here today, you. . . deep in my heart . . . when I practiced law I represented a lot of lawyers who got in trouble. And, you come saying I have made my mistakes, but now I want to change my life. And you know, if we . . . as a nation did not give people an opportunity after they've made mistakes to change their lives, a whole lot of people would not do very well.

I don't know where you go from here. As I sat here and I listened to both sides, I just felt as if . . . and you know. . . people are now using my words, that they took from me, that didn't give me any credit. We are better than this. . . . We really are. As a country, we are so much better than this.

And, you know, I told you, and for some reason, Mr. Cohen, I tell my children, I say, "When bad things happen to you, do not ask the question 'Why did it happen to me?' Ask the question 'Why did it happen for me?'" I don't know why this is happening for you. But it's my hope that a small part of it is for our country to be better. If I hear you correctly, it sounds like you're crying out for a new normal—for us getting back to normal. It sounds to me like you want to make sure that our democracy stays intact.

The one meeting I had with President Trump, I said to him 'the greatest gift that you and I, Mr. President, can give to our children, is making sure we give them a democracy that is intact. A . . . democracy better than the one we came upon. And I'm hoping that, the things you said today will help us again to get back there.

You know, I mean come on now. I mean, when you got, according to the *Washington Post*, our president has made at least 8,718 . . . false or misleading statements. That's stunning. That's not what we teach our children. I don't teach mine that. And, for whatever reason, it sounds like you got caught up in it. You got caught up in it. You got caught up in it.

And, some kind of way, I hope that you will, I know that it's painful going to prison. I know it's got to be painful being called a rat. And let me explain, a lot of people don't know the significance of that, but I live in the inner city of Baltimore, all right? And when you call somebody a rat, that's one of the worst things you can call them because when they go to prison, that means a snitch. I'm just saying. And so, the president called you a rat. We're better than that! We really are. And I'm hoping that all of us can get back to this democracy that we want, and that we should be passing on our children so they can do better than what we did.

So you wonder whether people believe you—I don't know. I don't know whether they believe you. But the fact is, that you've come, you have your head down, and this has got to be one of the hardest things that you could do.

Let me tell you the picture that really, really pained me. You were leaving the prison, you were leaving the courthouse, and, I guess it's your daughter, had braces or something on. Man that thing, man that thing hurt me. As a father of two daughters, it hurt me. And I can imagine how it must feel for you. But I'm just saying to you—I want to first of all thank you. I know that this has been hard. I know that you've faced a lot. I know that you are worried about your family. But this is a part of your destiny. And hopefully this portion of your destiny will lead to a better, a better, a better Michael Cohen, a better Donald Trump, a better United States of America, and a better world. And I mean that from the depths of my heart.

When we're dancing with the angels, the question we'll be asked: In 2019, what did we do to make sure we kept our democracy intact? Did we stand on the sidelines and say nothing? . . .

And I'm tired of statements saying . . . people come in here and say "Oh, oh this is the first hearing." It is not the first hearing. The first hearing was with regard to prescription drugs. Remember, a little girl, a lady sat there . . . . Her daughter died because she could not get $330 a month in insulin. That was our first hearing. Second hearing: H.R. 1, voting rights, corruption in government. Come on now. We can do more than one thing. And we have got to get back to normal. With that, this meeting is adjourned.